THE GAMBLERS

by Val Smith

SAMUEL FRENCH, INC.
45 West 25th Street   NEW YORK 10010
7623 Sunset Boulevard HOLLYWOOD 90046
LONDON   TORONTO

To Michael

And a special thanks to Larry H.

IMPORTANT BILLING AND CREDIT
REQUIREMENTS

All producers of THE GAMBLERS *must* give credit to the Author of the Play in all programs distributed in connection with performances of the Play and in all instances in which the title of the Play appears for purposes of advertising, publicizing or otherwise exploiting the Play and/or a production. The name of the Author *must* also appear on a separate line, on which no other name appears, immediately following the title, and *must* appear in size of type not less than fifty percent the size of the title type.

In addition, the following credit must also listed in all programs and advertising used in connection with performances:

"Originally produced by The American Stage Company, James N. Vagias, Executive Producer."

THE GAMBLERS won the 1992 Mid-South Playwrights Competition and received a non-Equity production at the Circuit Playhouse/ Playhouse on the Square (Jackie Nichols, Artistic Director) in Memphis, Tennessee in April, 1992. It had its World Premiere at American Stage Company in Teaneck, New Jersey, where it opened on January 15, 1993. It was directed by Terence Lamude, with scenic design by Harry Feiner, costumes by Greg Barnes, lighting by Adam Silverman, sound design by Tom Gould, with Jennifer Plate as production stage manager and James N. Vagias as Executive Producer.

The cast was as follows:

EUGENIE O'BANNON ....Ann Crumb
JOSEPH .... Kevin N. Davis
JACKSON JOHN HAYES .... Jack Hallett
GERHARDT .... Terry Layman
TITUS O'BANNON .... Geoff Pierson
GEORGE CROSSMAN................Tom Whyte

CHARACTERS

Jackson John Hayes — A reverend, by turns ominous, erudite, devilish, and kind.

Eugenie O'Bannon — The planter's wife, beautiful and eccentric.

George Crossman — The gambler's capper, handsome and knows it, young with some rough edges.

Titus O'Bannon — A planter, strong, old, and vicious.

Joseph — A boat's steward, dapper and smart.

Gerhardt — A government deputy, a strong believer in right and wrong and nothing in between.

TIME and PLACE

Late summer sometime just prior to the Civil War.

Passenger-deck staterooms, saloon, the stalls, the main and hurricane decks of a sidewheeler making its return down the Mississippi from St. Louis to New Orleans.

THE GAMBLERS

ACT I

Scene 1

LIGHTS UP. The O'Bannon stateroom. A bed, a table with a chair. On the table, a bowl and pitcher, a mirror, a brush. Clothing is slung over the chair. MRS. O'BANNON and CROSSMAN recline in each other's arms on the bed, partially dressed—they already have made love. The sound of the boat's PADDLES beneath. A ship's BELL chiming.

CROSSMAN. I should go.

MRS. O'BANNON. We have time.

CROSSMAN. I have to go. (*CROSSMAN makes a movement away from her toward his clothing.*)

MRS. O'BANNON. Two o'clock. I'll wager I know exactly what Mr. O'Bannon is doing at this very moment.

(*As SHE describes the scene, the LIGHT comes up on another part of the stage. MR. O'BANNON, seated at a table in the saloon, follows the actions described.*)

MRS. O'BANNON. He's drunk his second afternoon pick-me-up. He is reading the paper. Or rather he's looking at the pictures and the selling price of cotton, the only two things he ever looks at. If something annoys him, he'll spit. (*O'BANNON spits.*) And if he's pleased, which he

7

will be since he made a profit, he'll snort. (*O'BANNON snorts.*) He'll take out his watch. Blow his nose. Look to see if anything interesting emerged. (*O'BANNON does.*) Then, oh, say, for another three-quarters of an hour, Mr. O'Bannon will sit, musing about why bowler hats are shaped the way they are. After that, his ascent to the hurricane deck for the usual "survey" of the river. A smoke. A stroll to keep the bourbon from "settlin' in the joints." And then, for the umpteenth time, he'll go down to the main deck to stare at his new thoroughbred. Just in case it had a notion to jump the guards and swim away to a happier life.

CROSSMAN. Don't like him much.

MRS. O'BANNON. My husband is a man of predictable habits.

CROSSMAN. My habit is never to be caught pants down in a married lady's stateroom.

MRS. O'BANNON. Don't tell me you're scared.

CROSSMAN. No. Lord, it's hot in here.

MRS. O'BANNON. Wait.

(*MRS. O'BANNON pours water from the pitcher into a bowl. CROSSMAN sits on the bed. SHE sponges his bare back.*)

MRS. O'BANNON. We should open the transom. That would be risky though, wouldn't it? (*SHE sponges his chest. SHE finishes. From the pocket of his jacket, SHE takes a silver card case. SHE tosses the case to him.*) You're no cheese salesman. For which I am very thankful.

CROSSMAN. Lots of gentlemen carry cards. Don't know many ladies who go through their pockets though.

MRS. O'BANNON. I would wager you are not acquainted with many ladies.
CROSSMAN. Pick one. Don't let me see it.

(*SHE does. CROSSMAN shuffles the deck.*)

CROSSMAN. Put it back. Anywhere.

(*SHE does. CROSSMAN shuffles again.*)

CROSSMAN. Now cut.

(*SHE does. HE takes a card from the top of the deck and shows her.*)

CROSSMAN. That the card?
MRS. O'BANNON. No.
CROSSMAN. (*HE takes the next card.*) That the one?
MRS. O'BANNON. No.
CROSSMAN. Hmmmmmm. Ah. Aha. (*HE draws the card out from the front of her bodice and shows her.*)
MRS. O'BANNON. Clever boy.
CROSSMAN. I know lots of card tricks. Don't mean I'm not a cheese salesman.
MRS. O'BANNON. But you aren't. Are you?
CROSSMAN. Oh, Mrs. O'Bannon, you scare the pants right off me.

(*LIGHTS DOWN on CROSSMAN and MRS. O'BANNON.*)

Scene 2

LIGHTS UP on MR. O'BANNON. REV. HAYES enters, pauses, deciding whether to approach O'Bannon. HE decides.

HAYES. Mind if I sit, sir?

(O'BANNON gestures. HAYES sits. O'BANNON spits. HAYES flips through the newspaper.)

HAYES. Now here's a thing. (*Reading.*) "Five years ago today saw the terrible tragedy of the *Louisiana* in which that proud steamer exploded her boilers at the foot of Gravier Street, New Orleans. Packets berthed on either side were leveled to the water and people over two hundred yards away were sliced to bits by flying debris. A twelve-foot beam demolished a coffee house two blocks over. A piece of metal cut a wharf mule in halves." Makes you think, don't it?

(O'BANNON takes out his watch, looks at it, replaces it, and spits.)

HAYES. Yes sir. Makes *me* think. Here we are, floatin' down this mighty river. Enjoying God's bounteous pleasures. And any minute, we could all be blown to spit.

(JOSEPH the steward appears.)

JOSEPH. Another, sah?

O'BANNON. Yes.
JOSEPH. You, sah?
HAYES. Believe I will. A nice cool julap.

(JOSEPH exits.)

HAYES. Dirt in a valve. Thin spot on a boiler. Engineer lays on that steam. And—straight to perdition. A mule cut in clean halves. Why, there's a whole sermon right in that.

O'BANNON. You are a preacher, sir?

HAYES. I am. Reverend Jackson John Hayes, sir. Of Cairo. On my way to the Crescent City.

O'BANNON. Titus O'Bannon.

HAYES. You look like a planter to me, sir. I can see you're wondering how I knew that.

O'BANNON. Not necessarily.

HAYES. Well sir, was your mustacios. No one but a planter would care for his mustachios just so. They lack the extreme measures which clearly identify the politician and the pint-sized bureaucrat. All that waxy stuff, torturin' 'em out to here. No sir, a planter treats his mustacios much as he does his crops. Reasonable harvests. Yet always a little roughness left round the edges. None of that vain artificiality for you, sir. My compliments.

O'BANNON. You always go around divining men's occupations by their mustacios?

HAYES. My duty, sir, as a preacher is to assess the state of men's souls. Since a soul is shaped by character and occupation, a preacher, a good one, should be able to gauge both. Take that man over there. What do you think he's about?

O'BANNON. Which?

HAYES. The young dandy.

O'BANNON. Sharper if I ever saw one.

HAYES. That is young Adam Johnson, second youngest son of my good friend, Judge Caleb Johnson of Cairo, Illinois. Oh, but he *is* suspect. Stupidity sits on him like a halo, don't you think? Mark my words, he'll be out that diamond stickpin 'fore we pass Vicksburg.

O'BANNON. What about that man there? Rough-looking character.

HAYES. A cowman by the curvature of his shins. A Texan certainly. Keeps missin' the spittoon.

O'BANNON. And that fella? Reading the paper?

HAYES. What do you make of him?

O'BANNON. Looks like an official. An underwriter maybe. Government-type.

HAYES. Look again. Anything exceptional about him?

O'BANNON. Looks entirely respectable to me.

HAYES. Indeed. No respectable person looks *that* respectable. There's your gambler, sir. A sharper and a cheat, by my reckoning.

O'BANNON. Go on!

(JOSEPH has brought the drinks.)

HAYES. I'd stake my Bible on it. Or the price of a drink.

O'BANNON. For the price of a drink I can stand it. Steward, go over to that man with the spectacles and ask him what he does for a living. Tell him it's in the service of a friendly wager.

JOSEPH. That man, sah? That's Mr. Gerhardt. Government deputy. Rides with us all the time.
O'BANNON. A government deputy.

(HAYES lays out some coins which JOSEPH takes. JOSEPH exits. A silence during which the MEN drink.)

HAYES. And the mighty are brought low.
O'BANNON. Uh-huh.
HAYES. God's retribution for being too prideful of my talents.
O'BANNON. You don't think the Lord looks askance at wagering?
HAYES. Oh no, sir. I find Him most forgiving on that score. Did not Abraham risk his son? And the Lord rewarded him.
O'BANNON. Didn't reward Adam ner Eve.
HAYES. True. But they were not guided by His will when they bit that apple. Sucker bet. If you examine the Good Book, you'll find God often speaks his will through wagers. By lot the land of Canaan was divided; by lot Saul was marked out for the Hebrew kingdom; and by lot Jonah was discovered to be the cause of the storm.
O'BANNON. Uh-huh.
HAYES. Don't misunderstand me, sir. I don't approve of sin. But neither do I believe men can entirely divest themselves of it. Those who try, well, they're bucking God surely. No, I say the man who knows what his vices are, keeps to them in moderation, will find he can govern them the better. Total denial is folly—the sin of pride. Tolerance is my rule. In myself as in others.

O'BANNON. Yet there are plenty of things a man should not tolerate.

HAYES. Oh?

O'BANNON. Bourbon is settlin' in the joints. Past time for my stroll.

HAYES. I'd be honored to join you, sir. Lead on.

(HAYES and O'BANNON rise, and exit.)

Scene 3

LIGHTS UP on MRS. O'BANNON and CROSSMAN. CROSSMAN rises and moves to finish dressing.

CROSSMAN. Now what time is it?

MRS. O'BANNON. Stop worrying.

CROSSMAN. I have an appointment.

MRS. O'BANNON. To sell some cheese?

CROSSMAN. As a matter of fact. Go on. Go on and laugh.

MRS. O'BANNON. I'm not laughing. I'm angry with you.

CROSSMAN. Why?

MRS. O'BANNON. It's a poor excuse.

CROSSMAN. Man's gotta earn a living.

MRS. O'BANNON. And we both know how this man earns his living. Your secret is safe with me. Why won't you admit it?

CROSSMAN. Admit what?

MRS. O'BANNON. Suppose I were to tell you that Mr. O'Bannon made quite a profit on his cotton up North. Thousands of dollars. All of it right here. On this boat.

CROSSMAN. He in the market for cheese?

MRS. O'BANNON. Hardly. And then of course, there's that new thoroughbred one deck down. Must be worth something.

CROSSMAN. So?

MRS. O'BANNON. I'm simply telling you. So you'll know.

CROSSMAN. And why would I want to?

MRS. O'BANNON. Thought it might interest you.

CROSSMAN. I really do have to go.

MRS. O'BANNON. (*Stops him dressing.*) You disappoint me, George.

CROSSMAN. Really? My, you are hard to please.

MRS. O'BANNON. I don't mean *that*. Something tells me, you've done that more than a few times. I'm talking about real risk.

CROSSMAN. All right then. Only to please you. My admission. Yes, indeed, I gamble; I am indeed a gambler. I spend my whole time tempting innocents. When I'm not busy soiling the purity of young blossoms like yourself, I am diddling dandies and the local rubes. I take their money, the farm, everything right on down to their shoe leather. They are totally, absolutely, irretrievably dishonored. And broke, too.

MRS. O'BANNON. You snake, you.

CROSSMAN. Well, can't say you weren't warned. Man or woman. Nobody's safe from my dastardly dastardliness. Widow's wedding rings. Silver rattles from the mouths of babes. Hey now, I got a whole mess of those.

And where I'm from, lady, men sweat at the mention of my name and womenfolk swoon in heaps at my toes. You got me pegged aright, Mrs. O'Bannon. I stand before you a thief, a cad, a scoundrel and an utter swine. A gambler. But—a damned handsome one.

MRS. O'BANNON. Spoken like a true cheese salesman.

CROSSMAN. You are a cruel woman.

MRS. O'BANNON. Get out.

CROSSMAN. What?

(MRS. O'BANNON has gathered up the cards. But does not give them to CROSSMAN who obviously wants them before he leaves.)

MRS. O'BANNON. You're in a such a hurry. Go. Get out.

CROSSMAN. Why—

MRS. O'BANNON. Nobody likes to be dismissed, George. You see how unpleasant it is.

I'm going to leave Mr. O'Bannon.

CROSSMAN. You have my sympathy and best wishes, Mrs. O'Bannon.

MRS. O'BANNON. I need your help to do it.

CROSSMAN. Look—

MRS. O'BANNON. No. You told me a story. I'll tell you one. It won't take long.

(*LIGHTS up on O'BANNON and HAYES. THEY are admiring O'Bannon's thoroughbred in the boat's paddock.*)

HAYES. That's what I'd call a *horse*!

O'BANNON. Yes.

HAYES. Must have cost a packet.

MRS. O'BANNON. Mr. O'Bannon's had another thoroughbred, you see. A prize filly.

O'BANNON. Animal like this. You don't talk money in the same breath.

MRS. O'BANNON. Now, he felt a great affection for this horse, fawned over it as though it were a child. Naturally his expectation was that such attentions would be reciprocated. Animals are simple creatures. They are more trusting than us.

HAYES. She's a beauty.

MRS. O'BANNON. But in their likes and dislikes, they can often be as capricious. The horse took apples from the trainer. Sugar from me. But it absolutely refused anything from the hand of my husband. Quite a picture. A man respected—feared even—in six counties, humbled by the whims of a horse.

HAYES. You plan on racing her, then?

O'BANNON. No.

HAYES. Too bad. Looks like a goer.

MRS. O'BANNON. But my husband is quite relentless when he sets his mind on something. And so, one day at the end of months of coaxing, Mr. O'Bannon was rewarded. The horse ate his apple. And as Mr. O'Bannon proudly walked his prize filly back toward the paddock, she turned and bit his hand. Hard. Just like that. I expected a holy fury. But my husband surprised us all. He laughed. A small, dry, little laugh I had never heard before.

HAYES. You plan to keep her for a saddle-horse then?

O'BANNON. Don't know.

MRS. O'BANNON. The very next day, he ordered the horse shut up. Neither watered nor fed. For as long as it took. It didn't take long.

HAYES. Breed mare maybe?

O'BANNON. Haven't decided.

MRS. O'BANNON. The final indignity.

O'BANNON. I just like to look at her.

HAYES. Proportion, strength, spirit, grace. A sermon on four legs. Yes sir.

MRS. O'BANNON. It was a message, you see. For me.

(LIGHTS down on O'BANNON and HAYES.)

MRS. O'BANNON. That is why you must help me. Take Mr. O'Bannon for all the money you can win from him. There'll be plenty for both of us.

CROSSMAN. Lots of gentlemen play cards, Jenny—

MRS. O'BANNON. They do. We will have to provide a distraction for your partner somehow. I'll have to think what.

CROSSMAN. (*Pause.*) Partner.

MRS. O'BANNON. The saloon, the barbershop, every deck there are men in groups, conducting business, passing the time. A lone woman taking the air, waiting for her husband, is hardly remarked upon. It took me some time to fathom it out.

You lose a lot to the same man.

CROSSMAN. Told you I was no professional.

MRS. O'BANNON. Nor a fool. I saw him give you money, George. He slipped it to you on the deck. After the game.

CROSSMAN. Charity's not a crime.

MRS. O'BANNON. Cheating is. You palm the cards, don't you? Well. Don't worry. No one knows.

Not the government deputy certainly. Not yet anyway.

CROSSMAN. Ha!

MRS. O'BANNON. How much of a cut do you get, George? Didn't seem like much of one to me.

CROSSMAN. I told you—

MRS. O'BANNON. Is it a fair one? In your estimation.

CROSSMAN. Why don't you just poison the old coot and be done with it?

(Pause.)

MRS. O'BANNON. I have thought of it. Who in my position wouldn't? But the truth, and you can believe this or no, George, is that I would like to keep what small amount of humanity I have left. *(Pause.)* I just want to get away from him. Somewhere he won't find me. I'll need money to do that.

CROSSMAN. Too bad you picked the wrong man.

MRS. O'BANNON. No, I didn't.

You don't like the good reverend. You could work alone. So why, I ask myself, do you stay with him? Fear?

CROSSMAN. *(Angry.)* I'm not afraid of him.

MRS. O'BANNON. And I believe you. I do.

(Pause.)

CROSSMAN. So. Got it all planned out.

MRS. O'BANNON. While we were up North, an acquaintance offered my husband a business opportunity in the West. My husband turned the man down flat. I, on the other hand, thought it a sound venture.

You find that amusing?

CROSSMAN. I find this whole damn thing comical. (*Pause.*) You want me to keep your husband from knowing who bit him? That's what you want?

MRS. O'BANNON. I would prefer he not know he's been bitten at all.

CROSSMAN. And you trust me to give you—

MRS. O'BANNON. Half.

CROSSMAN. My partner's not stupid.

MRS. O'BANNON. We'll think of something.

(*LIGHTS DOWN as MRS. O'BANNON puts the cards in CROSSMAN's hand.*)

Scene 4

LIGHTS UP on REV. HAYES and O'BANNON on hurricane deck.

HAYES. Are you certain it is no imposition?

O'BANNON. My wife will be pleased to have the company.

HAYES. Then I'd be happy to oblige.

O'BANNON. Ah. Look at the time. (*O'BANNON moves to exit.*)
HAYES. (*Calling after.*) Thank you, sir. I'll be there.

(*CROSSMAN approaching nearly collides with O'BANNON on his exit. O'BANNON is irritated but continues off.*)

HAYES. Hallo there.
CROSSMAN. Afternoon, Reverend.
HAYES. A pretty sight. Lazy afternoon on the river.
CROSSMAN. Yes.
HAYES. Warm haze over everything. Faint scent of smoke from the banks. Ah.
CROSSMAN. Yes.
HAYES. Late afternoon's best time for fishing, my daddy used to say. Everything's dozing. Don't even need a hook. Just reach in and scoop 'em up.
CROSSMAN. Uh huh.
HAYES. You're wet through.
CROSSMAN. Took a rest. Cabin was hot.
HAYES. Don't much care for naps myself. Might miss something. I prefer to be up and around.
Mr. Gerhardt, sir.
GERHARDT. Reverend.

(*REV. HAYES smiles and tips his hat as GERHARDT passes by and nods. CROSSMAN follows suit. GERHARDT lingers at some distance.*)

HAYES. Mr. Gerhardt. Government Deputy.
CROSSMAN. Oh.

HAYES. On board to protect God's seedlings from those Devil's Aphids, Blackleg Scourge known as gamblers. Seems there was a virtual infestation and they called in the law. They haven't touched you, have they?

CROSSMAN. The law?

HAYES. Gamblers.

CROSSMAN. Oh. No.

HAYES. Must be doing his job.

CROSSMAN. Must be.

HAYES. What line you say you were in?

CROSSMAN. Cheese drummer.

HAYES. Oh yes. Any prospects?

CROSSMAN. Not in this heat.

HAYES. I have an invitation to sup with a gentleman this evening. You should come along, George. Widen your circle of acquaintances.

CROSSMAN. Well, I don't know—

HAYES. Nothing to know, George.

CROSSMAN. I have another engagement.

HAYES. Oh. Well then.

Might I be so bold to ask with whom you are suppin'?

CROSSMAN. A friend.

HAYES. I see. Lady-friend is it?

CROSSMAN. —Business. Potential. Maybe.

HAYES. You do have some prospects. Good. We'll join you.

CROSSMAN. This is a private matter.

HAYES. (*Pause.*) Might as well talk to the air—

CROSSMAN. —I'll get out of it—

HAYES. Nevermind that now. The gent's wife will be along. Your lady friend will have somebody to talk to. I expect you'll find that a relief.

CROSSMAN. What time you going down?

HAYES. Eight o'clock. Sharp. Mr. O'Bannon's the punctual type.

CROSSMAN. I'll see what I can arrange.

HAYES. You do that now. You do that.

(HAYES exits. CROSSMAN wipes his face with his handkerchief. GERHARDT approaches.)

GERHARDT. Everything all right, sir?

CROSSMAN. What? Yes. Quite alright! Thank you!

GERHARDT. I merely asked—

CROSSMAN. —And I gave you an answer, I believe.

GERHARDT. You did. It was a friendly inquiry, sir. Nothing more. You seemed—

CROSSMAN. —It is not friendly to poke into matters not of your concern. If you have business of your own, I suggest you attend to it. Good day, sir!

(CROSSMAN exits. LIGHTS DOWN slowly on an astonished GERHARDT.)

Scene 5

LIGHTS UP on O'BANNON and MRS. O'BANNON. O'BANNON approaches her. SHE turns away.

MRS. O'BANNON. I'm dressing.

O'BANNON. Plenty of time.

(O'BANNON turns her face towards his. SHE moves away.)

MRS. O'BANNON. It's stifling in here.
O'BANNON. No wonder. You got the transom closed.
MRS. O'BANNON. I wanted some quiet.
Are you going to wear that coat?
O'BANNON. Of course.
MRS. O'BANNON. If you must.
O'BANNON. I must. I like it.
How was your siesta?
MRS. O'BANNON. Hot. Not very restful.
O'BANNON. Should have opened the transom.
MRS. O'BANNON. I wanted some quiet.
O'BANNON. Pilot says we're ahead of schedule.
MRS. O'BANNON. That's nice.
O'BANNON. Real talker, that pilot. Got this story about an underground river. Mirror image of this one, only underground, says he. That's where the whirlpools lead down to.
MRS. O'BANNON. Makes sense.
O'BANNON. Tells me he knows of a steamer got caught in a whirlpool. Sucked it right down. Never found the wreck nor nary one of the passengers.
MRS. O'BANNON. That's comforting.
O'BANNON. Pilot says the boat's down there yet. Going up and down the ghost river. All the men and women still there, hangin' on to the guards, hopin' to reach home. Quiet nights, he can hear them wailin' and cryin'. Down there in the dark.
MRS. O'BANNON. You're trying to frighten me.
O'BANNON. Ha, ha. Damn load of rot you ask me.

MRS. O'BANNON. Please. Not the floor.

(MR. O'BANNON spits into a hanky.)

O'BANNON. Company for supper.
MRS. O'BANNON. Oh?
O'BANNON. A reverend. Met him this afternoon.
MRS. O'BANNON. A reverend. Really?
O'BANNON. You're fond of talkers. You'll like him.
MRS. O'BANNON. What do you know about him?
O'BANNON. From Cairo. Going to New Orleans. Likes to talk.
MRS. O'BANNON. You should be careful of striking up acquaintances with total strangers, Titus.
O'BANNON. He's a reverend.
MRS. O'BANNON. What church?
O'BANNON. I don't know.
MRS. O'BANNON. What's his business in New Orleans?
O'BANNON. Didn't ask.
MRS. O'BANNON. You don't seem to know very much about him.
O'BANNON. I wasn't that interested.
MRS. O'BANNON. I suppose we'll be mired with the good reverend for the entire evening.
O'BANNON. You said you wanted company. I got you some.
MRS. O'BANNON. Endless anecdotes of provincial parish life. I'd hoped we'd meet someone more—intriguing than that.
O'BANNON. Intriguing—rot!

Wear the pearls.

MRS. O'BANNON. Pearls are for funerals. They're bad luck.

O'BANNON. I like them.

MRS. O'BANNON. They don't go with the dress.

O'BANNON. (*Fastens the pearl necklace around his wife's neck.*) There. Looks fine.

(*THEY look in the mirror together. O'BANNON notices something.*)

MRS. O'BANNON. What is it?

O'BANNON. You think my mustacios are too rough?

(*LIGHTS DOWN on MR. and MRS. O'BANNON.*)

Scene 6

Sound of the boat's PADDLES. A ship's clock CHIMES seven o'clock. LIGHTS UP on CROSSMAN doing coin tricks in the saloon.

JOSEPH. That's good. Do that again.

(*CROSSMAN does.*)

CROSSMAN. Another drink.

JOSEPH. Yes sah.

CROSSMAN. What's your name?

JOSEPH. Joseph.

CROSSMAN. You like games of chance, Joseph?
JOSEPH. Nope. Do that again.

(CROSSMAN does.)

JOSEPH. How you do that?
CROSSMAN. It's a secret. You keep a secret Joseph?
JOSEPH. Surely.

(CROSSMAN does it again.)

CROSSMAN. Figured it out yet?
JOSEPH. Nope.
CROSSMAN. Want me to tell you?
JOSEPH. Yes, I do.
CROSSMAN. If you can tell me we're docking at one o'clock tomorrow morning, I can tell you how it's done.
JOSEPH. We dock tomorrow afternoon.
CROSSMAN. Can't tell you the secret then.
JOSEPH. Do it again.
CROSSMAN. What if you could tell me we was pulling into shore, say, 'bout midnight for more wood. What if you could do that?
JOSEPH. I could. But we ain't.
CROSSMAN. But what if you could—and we was?
JOSEPH. I don't know. Pilot particular about his schedule.

(CROSSMAN produces a bill. The bills he produces, HE will place in a stack on the table.)

CROSSMAN. Tell me about the pilot's schedule now.

JOSEPH. Captain's got a bet going that he get to New Orleans heada time—

(*CROSSMAN produces another bill.*)

JOSEPH. Pilot's gonna need more wood though. Prob'ly.

(*CROSSMAN produces another bill.*)

JOSEPH. Way he's pilin' it inta that boiler. 'Most a certainty.

CROSSMAN. Why don't you like games of chance, Joseph?

JOSEPH. Too chancy.

CROSSMAN. That's right. Why you should never play unless you're good at it. Unless you have an edge. And the stakes are worth it.

JOSEPH. Yes sah.

CROSSMAN. Or unless you're playing just for plain old amusement. No harm in that, is there?

JOSEPH. No sah.

CROSSMAN. (*Produces a deck of card.*) Old Monongehela. There's a fine drink. I'll need some.

JOSEPH. Old Monongehela. Yes sir.

CROSSMAN. And a deck of cards. This deck. You've never seen this deck before in your life.

JOSEPH. Just went blind.

CROSSMAN. (*Dividing up bills.*) This is for the pilot. This is for when cards are requested. And this— (*CROSSMAN puts the remaining money in his coat.*)— this is for when the boat stops. At midnight.

JOSEPH. Sah?
CROSSMAN. Yes?
JOSEPH. The secret.
CROSSMAN. When the boat stops, Joseph. Secret for secret.

(LIGHTS DOWN on CROSSMAN at the bar.)

Scene 7

JOSEPH prepares a table in the saloon as REV. HAYES, MR. and MRS. O'BANNON move to go into supper. They are met on the deck by MR. GERHARDT.

GERHARDT. Mr. O'Bannon! I did manage to find the Captain, sir. He says there should be time enough to exercise your animal tomorrow when we dock. I would have mentioned it this afternoon in the saloon only you and the reverend—
O'BANNON. Oh. Yes. Reverend Hayes. My wife. Mr. Gerhardt.
MRS. O'BANNON. —the government deputy.
GERHARDT. A fellow traveler, m'am.
I won't detain you from your meal then. Oh, I'd avoid the beef. A mite—ripe, you know. Good evenin'.

(O'BANNON, HAYES, MRS. O'BANNON exit to dining room. GERHARDT exits in the opposite direction.)

Scene 8

HAYES, O'BANNON, MRS. O'BANNON seat themselves at table. JOSEPH in attendance.

HAYES. You and Mr. Gerhardt are acquainted?
O'BANNON. Your friend is late.
HAYES. He said he would be here.
MRS. O'BANNON. Perhaps your friend has changed his mind?
HAYES. Was perspiring like Niagara this afternoon.
MRS. O'BANNON. Oh dear.
MR. O'BANNON. What sort of work does your friend do, Reverend?
HAYES. He's a cheese salesman, sir.
O'BANNON. Could have sent word. Stomach thinks my throat's been cut.

(CROSSMAN enters.)

HAYES. Here he is. You're late.
CROSSMAN. My apologies.

(HAYES and O'BANNON stand for introductions.)

HAYES. Mr. and Mrs. O'Bannon. My tardy friend, Mr. George Crossman.
MRS. O'BANNON. Mr. Crossman.
CROSSMAN. Sir. M'am.
O'BANNON. Let's eat.

(ALL sit. O'BANNON signals Joseph to begin serving.)

O'BANNON. Anything but the beef.

JOSEPH. Sorry, sah. Beef's all that's left.

MRS. O'BANNON. The Reverend tells us you're a cheese drummer, Mr. Crossman.

CROSSMAN. Yes.

MRS. O'BANNON. Fascinating. Any particular kind?

CROSSMAN. I'm sorry?

MRS. O'BANNON. Does your company deal in any particular cheeses? *Specialités de maison*?

CROSSMAN. I don't believe so.

MRS. O'BANNON. Really? You don't sell Swiss?

CROSSMAN. Sorry?

MRS. O'BANNON. Swiss? Or cheddar? Or Gruyere. I adore Gruyere.

O'BANNON. Gru-what?

CROSSMAN. It's all just plain old cheese to us, m'am. Good old American cheese.

MRS. O'BANNON. Ah. How patriotic.

O'BANNON. Any money in it?

CROSSMAN. For me, you mean?

O'BANNON. Well, there ain't for me.

CROSSMAN. Enough to get by, I guess.

HAYES. You should see Mr. O'Bannon's filly downstairs, George. She's a corker!

CROSSMAN. You plan on racing her, Mr. O'Bannon?

O'BANNON. No, I do not.

HAYES. Mr. O'Bannon has a fondness for beautiful things, George. For those who appreciate it, beauty merits admiration in its own right.

O'BANNON. Let's get to it.

(JOSEPH pours more wine. MRS. O'BANNON motions him to refill her glass. SHE drinks hers down.)

MRS. O'BANNON A bottle of champagne, please.
O'BANNON. What do you want with that stuff?
MRS. O'BANNON. I like it. I thought we might celebrate.
O'BANNON. Celebrate what?
MRS. O'BANNON. Nothing. I just felt like champagne.
O'BANNON. Champagne.
MRS. O'BANNON. Yes. You drink what you like. I prefer champagne. *(To Joseph.)* Bring it please.
O'BANNON. Fine. I'll not argue it now. Bring it.
JOSEPH. Yes, sah.

(O'BANNON starts to dig in. HAYES clears his throat. ALL bow heads.)

HAYES. Merciful God, we thank thee for this bountiful meal. Grant that we may show the same measure of generosity and kindness to each other that, in your great wisdom, you have bestowed upon us here.

(ALL set to but are interrupted by:)

HAYES. Lord, we are all sinners in your sight. We seek your understanding and ask your forgiveness for our transgressions, past and present—

(A pause and some confusion as to whether HAYES is finished.)

HAYES. —Guide us in your will, O Lord. Amen.

ALL. Amen.

MRS. O'BANNON. Nicely spoken, Reverend. What church did you say you were with?

HAYES. The Ouachita Baptist Church, m'am.

MRS. O'BANNON. I cannot say I've heard of it.

HAYES. I'd be surprised if you had. Just a small congregation. But what it lacks in numbers, it makes up for in spirit.

MRS. O'BANNON. Isn't that charming, Mr. O'Bannon? I always thought Baptists opposed alcoholic libation. Am I mistaken?

HAYES. No. *(HAYES sips his wine.)*

MRS. O'BANNON. But your congregation does not follow that particular rule.

O'BANNON. The Reverend is a tolerant man.

MRS. O'BANNON. My point was we wouldn't wish to offend.

O'BANNON. No chance of that.

HAYES. I was telling Mr. O'Bannon earlier, my principle in the matter of human frailty is one of tolerance. A little alcohol now and again. In moderation, of course. Where's the harm?

MRS. O'BANNON. Very commendable, Mr. Hayes. Don't you think, Mr. Crossman?

CROSSMAN. Oh. Surely.

(THEY eat in silence. JOSEPH has brought the champagne and poured it for MRS. O'BANNON.)

MRS. O'BANNON. To kindness, generosity—and tolerance. (*SHE takes a deep drink from her glass.*)

O'BANNON. Mrs. O'Bannon!

MRS. O'BANNON. Mr. O'Bannon?

HAYES. Champagne drunk too quickly brings on the vapours.

MRS. O'BANNON. Oh. Then I shall be more careful. More moderate.

O'BANNON. Damn right.

MRS. O'BANNON. Titus!

CROSSMAN. Sure is hot.

HAYES. Should have seen him this afternoon. You was wet through.

MRS. O'BANNON. Do you have a fever, Mr. Crossman? You look feverish. Don't you think so, Mr. Hayes? (*SHE pours herself another glass.*)

CROSSMAN. Your concern is appreciated, m'am, but I'm quite well.

MRS. O'BANNON. Perhaps it's love.

MR. O'BANNON. Perhaps is what "love?"

MRS. O'BANNON. Strong emotions, especially that of love, can result in fever.

CROSSMAN. I assure you I don't have a fever, m'am.

HAYES. I don't know. Dallying with ladies can be a strenuous business. So I'm told.

CROSSMAN. I was taking a nap, Reverend.

O'BANNON. Don't marry any of 'em.

MRS. O'BANNON. Mr. O'Bannon must mean you to learn from his example.

O'BANNON. That's not amusing, Mrs. O'Bannon.

MRS. O'BANNON. I was speaking in jest, Titus.

O'BANNON. I wouldn't marry a woman who dallied back. That's all that I meant.

CROSSMAN. I was takin' a nap, sir.

MRS. O'BANNON. And yet you married me.

O'BANNON. I courted you. I didn't dally. And neither did you. There's the difference.

MRS. O'BANNON. Excuse me, Mr. O'Bannon, but in some minds, there might be little difference between courting and dallying. Or, if there is, dallying might well lead to courting.

O'BANNON. Dallying is not honorable.

MRS. O'BANNON. Shame on you then, Mr. Crossman.

CROSSMAN. I was taking a nap!

O'BANNON. I never said that.

MRS. O'BANNON. Your statement implied Mr. Crossman's dallying was dishonorable.

O'BANNON. The man was taking a nap!

CROSSMAN. I was. Really!

HAYES. You're being teased, George.

MRS. O'BANNON. But suppose if poor Mr. Crossman *had* been dallying—

MR. O'BANNON. —Leave it alone, woman. Stop talking rubbish and let the man eat his supper. Take my advice, boy. Stay clear of 'em.

MRS. O'BANNON. The ladies, he means, Mr. Crossman. My husband has a quaint sense of humour. So dry you'd hardly notice to laugh.

O'BANNON. Be quiet and eat your food.

CROSSMAN. It surely is hot this evenin'.

MRS. O'BANNON. Some champagne?

(MRS. O'BANNON reaches for the champagne. MR. O'BANNON moves it out of reach.)

HAYES. You do look kinda pale, George. Glass of whiskey?

MRS. O'BANNON. Now there's a thought. Burn it out.

CROSSMAN. No thank you. I don't have a fever. I'm just hot!

(MRS. O'BANNON touches CROSSMAN's thigh under the table. Startled, HE has a coughing fit. HAYES motions for JOSEPH to come forward.)

JOSEPH. More wine, sah?

O'BANNON. No!

HAYES. Water.

JOSEPH. Yes, sah.

(JOSEPH exits. CROSSMAN continues to cough. HAYES claps him on the back.)

O'BANNON. Man can't even eat his supper in peace!

HAYES. Not to worry, m'am. He'll live.

CROSSMAN. Went down the wrong chute.

(JOSEPH has brought the water. CROSSMAN drinks. THEY eat in silence.)

O'BANNON. Ought to be in New Orleans in a few days. What's your purpose there, Reverend?

HAYES. My holy mission is to purchase a pipe organ.

MRS. O'BANNON. And I'd always heard that Baptists were averse to music.

O'BANNON. Mrs. O'Bannon, must you take issue with everything?

MRS. O'BANNON. I merely mentioned that I was under the impression that Baptists were averse to music.

HAYES. True.

O'BANNON. But his group ain't. Is they?

HAYES. No—

O'BANNON. There.

MRS. O'BANNON. Forgive me, Mr. Hayes. I fear I've been unduly argumentative. I didn't mean to give that impression.

HAYES. Not at all, Mrs. O'Bannon. Truth be told, some of our elder folk didn't take to the idea at all. They were overruled in the final vote, however.

MRS. O'BANNON. Very democratic, your congregation.

HAYES. Those opposed wouldn't put in a cent. I'll be looking for a bargain.

MRS. O'BANNON. What a pity. Titus, perhaps you might—

(O'BANNON coughs, then spits.)

HAYES. God will prevail, Mrs. O'Bannon. He usually does. Somehow.

O'BANNON. I'm finished. Steward!

JOSEPH. Sah?

O'BANNON. We're finished here. Brandies for the gentlemen.

MRS. O'BANNON. I found that a most flavourful supper.

O'BANNON. It is a mystery to me how you would know.

CROSSMAN. I thought it was good.

MRS. O'BANNON. Here I've been so bold as to tease you and I haven't even inquired if there is a Mrs. Crossman?

O'BANNON. That's no business of ours.

MRS. O'BANNON. I am trying to make amusing conversation.

O'BANNON. Well, don't.

CROSSMAN. My work keeps me fairly occupied, m'am.

O'BANNON. Mrs. O'Bannon, it's late. You should retire.

(JOSEPH has served the brandy. MRS. O'BANNON opens her fan and fans herself.)

MRS. O'BANNON. It's not late at all. And it's awfully warm in our cabin. No air whatever.

O'BANNON. It ain't gonna get any cooler talkin' about it.

MRS. O'BANNON. A stroll on the deck would be pleasant.

O'BANNON. I just got my brandy.

MRS. O'BANNON. Perhaps Mr. Crossman might benefit from a walk then.

O'BANNON. Reverend Hayes, would you mind assisting my wife in her wishes?

HAYES. Oh. Ah. Certainly. I'd be honored, sir.

MRS. O'BANNON. Mr. Crossman. A pleasure to have made your acquaintance. I trust we shall see you again. Titus, don't be long.

(HAYES and MRS. O'BANNON exit.)

Scene 9

O'BANNON. I apologize for my wife's peculiar behavior. What comes of reading romantic novels. Champagne.
CROSSMAN. Known Mr. Hayes long?
O'BANNON. No. You know him well, I take it.
CROSSMAN. Just this trip. Entertaining gentleman.
O'BANNON. Of a kind.
CROSSMAN. Likes to gamble. Preachers are funny that way though. Get 'em away from home.
O'BANNON. Not very good at it.
CROSSMAN. Oh, so you've played him a game?
O'BANNON. A wager. He lost.

(Pause.)

CROSSMAN. I think the good Reverend credits himself as being more worldly-wise than is actually the case. If you want my opinion.
O'BANNON. You won him as well.
CROSSMAN. Wasn't exactly difficult.
O'BANNON. No. I only gamble when I have a mind to.

CROSSMAN. (*Stifles a laugh.*) Yes. Pays to be cautious.

O'BANNON. Not many players can give me a good, fast game the way I like.

CROSSMAN. Oh.

O'BANNON. Planters I know, play like old women.

CROSSMAN. Funny. Never had that experience of planters in a game.

O'BANNON. You don't say.

CROSSMAN. Nature of the trade, I'd guess. If it ain't flood, it's hurricane. Or it's too cold. Too wet. Disease. Other planters who don't mind seeing you fail because it means more money for them. Yep. Tons of risk. I always found planters a formidable bunch at the table.

O'BANNON. For a drummer, you know a hell of a lot about farming.

CROSSMAN. Had one. Once.

O'BANNON. And now you're selling cheese.

CROSSMAN. Yeah.

O'BANNON. You gonna try and sell me some?

CROSSMAN. Need any?

O'BANNON. No.

CROSSMAN. Play you a game of poker.

O'BANNON. I don't think so.

CROSSMAN. You think I can't give you a game you'll like.

O'BANNON. You haven't got enough money to play me.

CROSSMAN. I might surprise you on that score.

O'BANNON. I play no limit.

CROSSMAN. Fine.

O'BANNON. This your own money you playing with?

CROSSMAN. I'm gratified, sir, but is that really your worry?

O'BANNON. Alright. Someplace private.

CROSSMAN. Mrs. O'Bannon. I understand.

O'BANNON. The Reverend. He's gonna hover around me for that damn pipe organ now every chance he gets. I know the type.

CROSSMAN. Yes. So do I.

O'BANNON. We'll use your room. (*O'BANNON signals Joseph.*) We'll be retiring to his cabin.

CROSSMAN. One thirteen.

O'BANNON. Bring us something to drink. And a fresh pack of cards.

JOSEPH. Yes sah.

O'BANNON. The Reverend comes back, tell him we turned in.

JOSEPH. Yes sah.

O'BANNON. Oh. And go on up to my cabin. Tell my wife her husband sends his best regards and she'll see him in his own sweet time. And take along a big piece of cheese with that message. Give her something to chew on.

JOSEPH. Yes sah.

(*CROSSMAN and O'BANNON exit.*)

Scene 10

JOSEPH clears the table. GERHARDT enters.

GERHARDT. Couple of friendly gents. The beef is not good, Joseph.

JOSEPH. No sah. Cook say he don't think you a government deputy at all.

GERHARDT. What's that supposed to mean?

JOSEPH. He say with your nose, you gotta be royalty. In disguise.

GERHARDT. You tell cook if I encounter that hunk of cow, or anything like it masquerading as supper again, he'll be out of a job.

JOSEPH. Yes sah.

GERHARDT. What's the purpose of all these lavish trappings if the food is not good, I'd like to know.

JOSEPH. Where else they gonna go for grub?

GERHARDT. That's not the point. It's not polite to poison the passengers.

JOSEPH. Yes sah.

GERHARDT. Unless somehow that *is* the point.

JOSEPH. Not for me, sah. I need the work.

GERHARDT. Quite right. You know, Joseph, I envy you your job.

JOSEPH. Oh, I doubt that.

GERHARDT. But I do. Set a plate. Polish a glass. Sweep a floor. Pour a drink. Simple, easily accomplished tasks.

JOSEPH. Ah-huh.

GERHARDT. Not at all like my work. They all know who I am, Joseph. I am being shunned like the cholera.

JOSEPH. Word travel quick on the river.

GERHARDT. I think the captain has had a hand in spreading the news.

JOSEPH. Now why would he do that?

GERHARDT. He informed me this morning that I needn't be so vigilant in the execution of my duty. He warned me off of making arrests. What do you make of that?

JOSEPH. Probably worried you scaring off the regular passengers.

GERHARDT. It's insanity.

JOSEPH. No, sah. It's a fact. You find most the passengers lose a few dollars being entertained, they don't mind. But you arrest the cheat, you make 'em look the public fool and that's a whole other story.

GERHARDT. The problem is, Joseph, that bringing cheats to justice is my job. Now, what I am to do, if I'm not to do my job?

JOSEPH. Enjoy the ride, I guess.

GERHARDT. It's an outrage. I've half a mind to report him.

JOSEPH. Who, sah? The captain? I wouldn't.

GERHARDT. Because he has connections. Yes, so he led me to understand.

JOSEPH. Got that far, did it?

GERHARDT. Yes, it did. We are at grave odds.

JOSEPH. People know who you is, that's not such a bad thing, Mr. Gerhardt. Sharpers'll stay out your way. That's some good.

GERHARDT. But they will continue to work, Joseph. And if someone ever does take it into their head to complain about being robbed, it will be easy enough to blame me. "Where was Gerhardt? He was enjoying the ride."

JOSEPH. Yes sah. Captain's a bad man to cross, sah. You gonna have to watch your back.

GERHARDT. Find some other way to discourage cheats.

(JOSEPH laughs.)

JOSEPH. Sorry, sah.
GERHARDT. No. Tell me.
JOSEPH. Well, sah. You got to understand how it is. You get in a game on this boat, you better know it's likely rigged. You find your own way to even up the odds. You be surprised how many regular passengers can look out for theyself.
GERHARDT. Free enterprise.
JOSEPH. Could see it thataway, yes sah.
GERHARDT. They deserve the beef.
JOSEPH. Yes sah.
GERHARDT. I'll need your help, Joseph.
JOSEPH. Sah?
GERHARDT. To watch my back. Another pair of eyes would be helpful. *(GERHARDT pushes a coin to JOSEPH.)* I'm not going to arrest anyone. Just— discourage potential trouble. Protect myself.
JOSEPH. I understand. Yes, sah. *(Takes the coin.)*
GERHARDT. Good man.

(LIGHTS DOWN.)

Scene 11

LIGHTS UP on HAYES. and MRS. O'BANNON on the hurricane deck.

MRS. O'BANNON. Look. The fog has come in.

HAYES. Comin' in awful thick. Pilot should pull to.

MRS. O'BANNON. A good pilot knows the river with his eyes closed. So Mr. O'Bannon tells me.

HAYES. Yes, well, even the best pilots have downed their boats. He should pull to. River's treacherous enough without fog.

We should be getting along to your cabin.

MRS. O'BANNON. Anxious you'll miss out on the brandy and cigars, Reverend?

HAYES. Not at all.

MRS. O'BANNON. You are polite. But I quite understand.

HAYES. Forgive me if I am direct, Mrs. O'Bannon, but do you have some cause to dislike me?

MRS. O'BANNON. Dislike you, Mr. Hayes? Why, no. I don't dislike you.

HAYES. Mistrust then.

MRS. O'BANNON. I am content that my husband trusts you.

HAYES. But you do not.

MRS. O'BANNON. My opinion hardly matters.

HAYES. On the contrary. I value your regard every bit as much as your husband's.

MRS. O'BANNON. Really.

HAYES. I happen to like brandy and cigars. I'm not pious enough?

MRS. O'BANNON. You do not resemble any reverend I've had occasion to know.

HAYES. Forgive me, Mrs. O'Bannon, but yours is a most conventional view of the clergy. You might be surprised to learn the number of our profession who do not conform to it. You might also find it surprising the number of regular folk who believe your pious, holier-than-holy preacher is either a tyrant, a fool, or a natural hypocrite. Usually all three. But my flaws being evident and relatively minor, my brethren have had no trouble accepting them. If anything, they trust me all the more because of them. Gives us something to talk about.

MRS. O'BANNON. I shouldn't count on getting any donations from my husband, Mr. Hayes.

HAYES. I never hoped for such a thing, Mrs. O'Bannon.

MRS. O'BANNON. Good. Then you won't be disappointed.

HAYES. Mr. O'Bannon is a fortunate man to have a wife who is not only beautiful but protective of his interests. I admire that.

MRS. O'BANNON. Adding flattery to your list of flaws, Reverend?

HAYES. I am merely saying that Mr. O'Bannon doesn't credit your intelligence near enough.

MRS. O'BANNON. Suddenly, I feel so fortunate to be having this conversation.

HAYES. He works in mysterious ways.

MRS. O'BANNON. Ah. Look at it, all that whiteness. The most commonplace thing softened, transformed, made mysterious. And so quiet. Like nothing else exists on the face of the earth.

HAYES. It is kind of … lovely.

MRS. O'BANNON. (*Pause*.) And … really … damp. Shall we continue?

(*MRS.O'BANNON takes the arm of a disconcerted HAYES as THEY move off and LIGHTS slowly fade.*)

End of ACT I

ACT II

Scene 1

Crossman's stateroom. O'BANNON and CROSSMAN playing.

CROSSMAN. Call.

(O'BANNON throws down his cards. CROSSMAN does also.)

O'BANNON. Ah ha! A happy pair of monarchs. Kings over knaves.

(O'BANNON rakes in money from the center, leaving a couple of bills for ante. CROSSMAN antes for the next hand.)

O'BANNON. I can see why you failed as a farmer.
CROSSMAN. Luck ain't in my corner at the moment is all.
O'BANNON. Pray your luck changes, Crossman. I ain't paying your way home.
CROSSMAN. Don't expect you'll have to.
O'BANNON. Good. Because Titus O'Bannon never deserts. Once on a scent, he sticks to the end. Bitter though it may be. (*O'BANNON laughs.*) I'm thinking of Mrs. O'Bannon's face. We will see how well she likes cheese.

Why is it drummers always try to sell you something you don't want?

CROSSMAN. They mainly try to show you why you *should* want it.

O'BANNON. Well, no chance of that happening this century. I hate cheese.

CROSSMAN. Can't fault a man for trying to make a living.

O'BANNON. Way you're handing out the company profits, you may not have one for long.

CROSSMAN. I know what I'm doing.

O'BANNON. Uh huh. And if pigs get wings, we better never look up.

(CROSSMAN bets heavy. O'BANNON sizes him up, then calls. CROSSMAN loses.)

O'BANNON. Keep chasing those dreams, boy.

(LIGHTS DOWN.)

Scene 2

LIGHTS UP on O'Bannon stateroom. MRS. O'BANNON entering. HAYES hesitates to follow.

MRS. O'BANNON. Come in. Please.

HAYES. Mrs. O'Bannon, with your permission—

MRS. O'BANNON. Oh, but I cannot give you leave to go just yet, Mr. Hayes.

HAYES. You said you were weary.
MRS. O'BANNON. Of walking. Please.

(HAYES sits reluctantly.)

MRS. O'BANNON. Do you know Mr. O'Bannon is most impressed by your way with words.
HAYES. Is he?
MRS. O'BANNON. He said you were quite the yarn-spinner.
HAYES. That was kind. I guess.
MRS. O'BANNON. Oh, it was a compliment. Mr. O'Bannon is a miserable story-teller. Just dreadful. So he is envious of that talent in other people.
HAYES. Mrs. O'Bannon—
MRS. O'BANNON. Lord knows, he tries—
HAYES. M'am, I m afraid it's getting late—
MRS. O'BANNON. —But oh dear, he gets everything all jumbled up, or forgets crucial points—and he has this disgusting habit of spitting—
HAYES. Mrs. O'Bannon. Forgive me. I have to be getting along.
MRS. O'BANNON. You are bored.
HAYES. —No, no—
MRS. O'BANNON. —Yes, yes, you are. Bored. Bored. Bored. Bored to distraction.
HAYES. Not at all. It's merely—
MRS. O'BANNON. —I meant it, you know, when I said you don't resemble any reverend I've had occasion to know. You're a most original person, Mr. Hayes. I was just about to be intrigued. But if you must run away—
HAYES. —I'm not running away, m'am.

MRS. O'BANNON. Then don't.

HAYES. (*A beat. HAYES sits again.*) It's exceeding warm in here.

MRS. O'BANNON. Is it? It's far too damp out there. (*A beat.*) Do you think you will have success in finding a pipe organ? One you can afford?

HAYES. I imagine that is strictly in the Lord's hands.

MRS. O'BANNON. A matter of luck.

HAYES. We'd call it providence.

MRS. O'BANNON. Yes. So many things are. A matter of providence, I mean. Like meeting interesting new people. One never knows who one will encounter on a voyage. That's what makes travel so stimulating.

(*A beat.*)

HAYES. I really have to be going, m'am.

MRS. O'BANNON. You know, I've never met a reverend who played poker. And so expertly. Is your winning at cards also a matter of providence, Reverend? Or is it sheer skill? Or is it something else?

(*A beat. HAYES is understandably disturbed by this remark.*)

MRS. O'BANNON. Because if it's providence, why then, she certainly smiles on you, Mr. Hayes —
—Well, let's be accurate and say she practically grins from ear to ear! Oh dear me, Mr. O'Bannon would have no chance at all going up against that kind of divine intervention.

HAYES. I wasn't aware Mr. O'Bannon liked the cards.

MRS. O'BANNON. Now, there, that's surprising. I am surprised that you did not know. I'd have thought you would have.

HAYES. What are you saying?

MRS. O'BANNON. I am saying—

(A KNOCK at the door.)

MRS. O'BANNON. Who is it?

JOSEPH. (*O.S.*) Joseph, the steward, m'am. Delivery from Mr. O'Bannon.

MRS. O'BANNON. Come.

(JOSEPH enters, carrying a tray with a large slice of cheese on it.)

JOSEPH. Mr. O'Bannon said to send you up this cheese, m'am, and tell you he'd be along in his own time. That's whad he said to say.

MRS. O'BANNON. Oh. Wasn't that thoughtful? Such a gracious man. Even if he does have some disgusting habits.

Now you must stay, Mr. Hayes. Partake of my husband's generosity. I insist. Steward. A moment. (*MRS. O'BANNON has taken writing materials from the dressing table and prepares to write a note.*) Such a kind gesture deserves a prompt acknowledgement. (*SHE writes as LIGHTS TO HALF.*)

Scene 3

LIGHTS TO FULL on Crossman's stateroom. THEY play through the following.

CROSSMAN. So every four years, see, Old Man Ferguson'd toss his hat in the ring. And every four years, down he'd go to dismal defeat. This went on long as anybody could recall. And nobody knew *why* Ferguson wanted to be mayor. He just did. Man couldn't sling a speech to save his soul. But you knew it was leap year, 'cause there he'd be. Big sign on the side of his wagon:
"Vote For Ferguson—Before Ferguson Dies."

(A beat.)

O'BANNON. And?
CROSSMAN. And, finally, after about thirty years, it was like everybody in town said, "Ah-h hell. Why not?" Old Ferguson won by one vote.
Shock killed him.
I don't know what that says about determination. But it's scary. Ain't it?

(LIGHTS DOWN.)

Scene 4

LIGHTS UP FULL on O'Bannon stateroom. MRS. O'BANNON finishing letter. HAYES tries discreetly to glimpse its contents. SHE notices this and folds the letter quickly and seals it.

MRS. O'BANNON. There. (*Handing letter to Joseph.*) Deliver that to Mr. O'Bannon. It's important.
JOSEPH. Yes, m'am. (*JOSEPH exits.*)
HAYES. You were saying—
MRS. O'BANNON. Yes. I was saying that you can abandon your idea of getting my husband into a poker game so that you can steal his money, Mr. Hayes. If I must, I'll follow you all over this boat to prevent that happening.

(*A beat as HAYES takes in what she has said. HE laughs.*)

MRS. O'BANNON. You may find this amusing. But I tell you I *know* you are not what you pretend to be.
I saw you. I saw you cheating.
HAYES. (*A beat. HAYES is not amused.*) That is a very serious allegation—
MRS. O'BANNON. Do you deny it?
HAYES. Of course. It's ridiculous.
MRS. O'BANNON. I am a very keen observer. My eyesight is excellent.
HAYES. No doubt. What—exactly—was it that you saw?

(*A beat.*)

MRS. O'BANNON. Oh, well, you don't expect me to explain precisely how it was done! It's enough that it *was* done. How else could you have won so consistently? Even your friend, poor Mr. Crossman, lost money.

(HAYES laughs.)

MRS. O'BANNON. You can't fool me. I know what I saw.

HAYES. Forgive me for saying this, m'am, but—

MRS. O'BANNON. —And I intend to warn everyone. You'll be lucky to get a game with Mr. O'Bannon's horse by the end of this trip. Reverend.

HAYES. Mrs. O'Bannon. When one makes an accusation, especially one of such a serious nature, it is incumbent upon the accuser—you—to produce some shred of proof. You saw me win. Now, what's wrong with that? It doesn't mean I cheated at all. It means I had a run of luck.

MRS. O'BANNON. A matter of providence.

HAYES. Whatever—

MRS. O'BANNON. Perhaps Mr. Gerhardt will think differently.

HAYES. Mr. Gerhardt will require proof. He will not thank you. Nor will I if you attempt to damage my good name.

MRS. O'BANNON. People have to be protected.

(HAYES, disgusted, moves to leave.)

MRS. O'BANNON. I've summoned my husband.

HAYES. Yes. All that business with the letter, I know.

MRS. O'BANNON. He's coming here. And you must stay until he arrives and can determine an appropriate course of action.

HAYES. Madam. I have only one thing to say and that is: Horse. Manure.

MRS. O'BANNON. Very well. I will follow you. I'll hound you all over this boat if necessary!

HAYES. (*Turning abruptly.*) Why are you doing this?! Why are you so insistent on persecuting me?! What have you got against the clergy?!

MRS. O'BANNON. Clergy. Ho.

(*HAYES looks at MRS. O'BANNON. Though angry, HE contains it, and decides the best course is to humour her.*)

HAYES. Alright. Alright. I had hoped to join my good friend, George, who's probably wondering whether I dropped off the face of the earth. But I will stay. George'll just have to amuse himself. Which I am sure he is perfectly capable of doing. I will stay here until your husband arrives. At which time, we will resolve this matter, Mrs. O'Bannon, once and for all. Does that satisfy?

MRS. O'BANNON. Yes. Thank you.

(*HAYES sits. With a flourish, HE whacks off a piece of cheese and eats it. LIGHTS DOWN.*)

Scene 5

LIGHTS UP on JOSEPH on deck, peering at the outside of the Mrs. O'Bannon's letter. GERHARDT enters.

GERHARDT. Got anything for me, Joseph?

JOSEPH. What? Oh, no, Mr. Gerhardt. Lady just wants me to deliver this to her husband.

GERHARDT. Which lady is that?

JOSEPH. Mrs. O'Bannon.

GERHARDT. Ah, yes.

JOSEPH. On my way down to the stalls. I figure Mr. O'Bannon prob'ly down there looking at that horse again.

GERHARDT. I doubt he'll be down there.

JOSEPH. No?

GERHARDT. Anything else to report?

JOSEPH. No sah. Quiet this evening.

GERHARDT. Let me see the letter.

(GERHARDT takes it from an uneasy JOSEPH.)

JOSEPH. Mrs. O'Bannon entertaining a reverend.

GERHARDT. (*Reading.*) Whew! It would appear that the Reverend's company has put her in a decidedly ill-temper. I can understand that. Poor thing.

JOSEPH. I best get on.

GERHARDT. What do you know about Crossman?

JOSEPH. Sah?

GERHARDT. Mr. Crossman. You know, I'm beginning to have a real feeling about that fella.

JOSEPH. Don't know him, sah.

GERHARDT. You don't? Don't you? That's peculiar, Joseph. Seeing as how you delivered a bottle to his room just a half hour past. Also odd that you failed to notice Mr. O'Bannon who's also in there. Door's closed but it sounded to me like they got a game going.

Or didn't you want me to know about that?

JOSEPH. Well, sah, you asked me to report potential trouble. Far as I could see, nothing there for you to worry yourself over.

GERHARDT. Come on, Joseph. Did he pay you?

JOSEPH. No, sah.

GERHARDT. Whose cards they playing with?

JOSEPH. House.

GERHARDT. Who's winning?

JOSEPH. Mr. Gerhardt, you go bustin' up private games, you get yourself in real deep.

GERHARDT. We had an arrangement, remember? (*A beat.*) I got a feeling about Crossman.

JOSEPH. What you plannin' to do then?

GERHARDT. (*Looking out.*) Such an inhospitable landscape. Looked better in the fog. And the odour is none too savory either.

JOSEPH. Swamp smell like that.

GERHARDT. I wouldn't want to get off around here.

JOSEPH. No sah.

GERHARDT. No sah. I'd imagine it would be especially unhealthy for a free colored like yourself. (*A beat.*) You have family down here. Isn't that what you told me?

JOSEPH. Who knows where they is these days, Mr. Gerhardt.

GERHARDT. That's very sad. (*A beat.*) Difficult times we're going through. Very difficult. Hard to know who or what to trust anymore.

Pilot told me just last week they caught contraband slaves aboard *The Minotaur*. In a space no bigger hardly than a cotton bale. Hard to see how they could even—

JOSEPH. I stay clear that kind of thing.

GERHARDT. That's probably best.

JOSEPH. No, sah. Besides. We goin' south.

GERHARDT. So we are. (*A beat.*) We had an arrangement.

JOSEPH. Still do, Mr. Gerhardt. I just want to do my job. I got to do my job.

GERHARDT. (*Indicating the letter.*) Then go and do your job.

(*GERHARDT makes as if to give JOSEPH the letter. JOSEPH moves to take it. GERHARDT pulls it back.*)

GERHARDT. We'll give Crossman plenty of rope. One hour should be sufficient. Be prompt.

JOSEPH. Yes sah.

GERHARDT. (*Relinquishes the letter.*) Good. (*Offering a coin.*) Here.

(*JOSEPH takes it. GERHARDT moves off.*)

GERHARDT. I need a drink.

(*JOSEPH watches GERHARDT go. LIGHTS DOWN.*)

Scene 6

The O'Bannon stateroom. MRS. O'BANNON, sitting at one side of the table, is reading a romantic novel. HAYES seated at the opposite side, is reading the Bible. HAYES finishes the last piece of cheese. A clock CHIMES the hour. HAYES closes the Bible, stretches, and yawns. MRS. O'BANNON looks up. A beat.

HAYES. Mr. O'Bannon must have forgotten where he lives.

MRS. O'BANNON. He will be here.

HAYES. Yep. I expect any moment now, he'll come riding in on a turtle.

Probably getting cleaned out by some darn Methodist.

MRS. O'BANNON. Sarcasm is one of the lowest forms of humour.

HAYES. I have been in some incredible scrapes in my life, but this takes the ribbon. Held captive by a lovely but singularly—forgive me—whimsical woman. It's a unique experience for me.

Word gets out about *this*, I'll never live it down.

Not that I'm complaining, you understand.

MRS. O'BANNON. I'm so glad you're enjoying yourself.

HAYES. 'Course if a lady, even a particularly handsome one, were to send me a missive in the tone of the one that recently sailed out of here, I believe I would rather go face-down on an anthill after eating a peach than honor such a summons.

By the looks of it, your husband seems of a similar mind.

MRS. O'BANNON. How do you know what tone I used?

HAYES. Oh, I know what I saw. And I saw enough to get the tenor of the thing.

MRS. O'BANNON. If I let you leave, you'll find a way to ensnare Mr. O'Bannon.

HAYES. Ensnare? Ensnare? Let me see that. (*HAYES takes the book from her and reads*.) "Being the journal of one Esmeralda Clay. Whose sad life is herein recounted for the benefit of instructing innocents against the temptations of—beeda, beeda, beeda,—may be found to be as prevalent these days—beeda, beeda, beeda—strangers whose honeyed tongues and handsome demeanors belie—beeda, beeda— who coil about and ensnare—ensnare! the unsuspecting dove—" (*HAYES tosses down the book. Withering.*) Ensnare. Bilge.

MRS. O'BANNON. I'm at the end where she joins the convent and regrets her life of sin and degradation. But the rest is quite good. You may borrow it if you like.

HAYES. You know, Mrs. O'Bannon, I believe there's more to this situation than mere insanity.

MRS. O'BANNON. You're trying to make me angry. So I'll throw you out.

HAYES. It's a thought. But actually I am considering the pattern of your actions thus far. Your behavior at dinner, for an instance.

MRS. O'BANNON. What was the matter with my behavior at dinner?

HAYES. Your flirtatiousness—

MRS. O'BANNON. I beg your pardon!

HAYES. You should. Seemed to me an almost purposeful effort to vex your husband—

MRS. O'BANNON. It most certainly was not!

HAYES. —With what result? You were perhaps hoping for some other outcome, but he sends you away accompanied by a man he can trust. Whose character, as many will attest to, is above reproach.

MRS. O'BANNON. He is deceived in that, we know.

HAYES. Once in the privacy of your stateroom, my duty to him fulfilled, on the very precipice of departure, and I am accused of being a villain. A cheat.

MRS. O'BANNON. Quite right.

HAYES. On the flimsiest of evidence.

MRS. O'BANNON. Hardly. I've been watching you for weeks.

HAYES. Weeks? Weeks!

MRS. O'BANNON. In the saloon. Every afternoon, you were there. Plying your trade.

HAYES. Well, why didn't you denounce me then? Mr. Gerhardt couldn't have been far away.

MRS. O'BANNON. And create a public scene? Really.

HAYES. Before dinner then. You could have mentioned it to Gerhardt even then. Certainly you had ample time to warn your husband!

MRS. O'BANNON. I didn't wish to upset him! Why are you asking me all these questions?

HAYES. If I am the villain you say I am, you seem awful darn comfortable in keeping me around. If I had an ensnarer of innocent doves in my room, I'd be a little nervous. (*Beat.*) Come now, Mrs. O'Bannon. You know all of it is a fabrication. You were trying for somebody more the part—namely, George—but, bad luck—

providence, sorry—you ended up with me. Nevertheless you made up a silly story to keep me here. You summoned your husband in the hopes he would arrive. Perhaps be a little jealous. And possibly pay you a little better attention and respect than he has evidently done of recent.

Now. That's the truth.

It's the only logical explanation.

(MRS. O'BANNON looks up at him on the edge of tears. A beat.)

HAYES. *(A real question.)* Isn't it?

(LIGHTS DOWN.)

Scene 7

LIGHTS UP on Crossman's stateroom. O'BANNON is losing heavily.

CROSSMAN. Something the matter?
O'BANNON. Nothing. Indigestion.
CROSSMAN. Well. I feel just fine. What time is it?
O'BANNON. *(Checks his watch, then puts it away. A beat.)* Closing in on eleven. Why? Going somewheres?
CROSSMAN. Just wondered.

(A KNOCK. JOSEPH enters.)

JOSEPH. More refreshment, gentlemen?

CROSSMAN. In a while.

(*JOSEPH hovers.*)

O'BANNON. What is it?
JOSEPH. A letter for you, sah.

(*JOSEPH hands it to O'BANNON. O'BANNON reads it. HE is not pleased.*)

CROSSMAN. Bad news?
O'BANNON. Damnable woman. She's locked me out.
CROSSMAN. Mrs. O'Bannon?
O'BANNON. (*Reading.*) She entreats me to come at once. Or seek accommodation elsewhere.
She mistakes me for a servant.
CROSSMAN. (*Amused.*) Didn't like the cheese after all.

(*O'BANNON stands abruptly.*)

CROSSMAN. You're *not* going?
O'BANNON. Maybe I will. Maybe I'll just go up and kick the door the hell in.
JOSEPH. That be destruction of private property, sah.
O'BANNON. I think I will. Kick it the hell in.
CROSSMAN. Calm down. We got a fine game going here. Don't you want to take back your losses? Think about it now.
O'BANNON. I am thinking about it.
CROSSMAN. Pay her back by staying in the game.

O'BANNON. That what you'd do?
CROSSMAN. I would. But if you'd rather dance to her tune—

(*O'BANNON crushes the note and throws it at Crossman's feet.*)

CROSSMAN. Just tryin' to help.

(*O'BANNON exits.*)

CROSSMAN. Hey! Hey there! O'Bannon!
Hell, we ain't even finished the hand.
JOSEPH. Left his money on the table.
CROSSMAN. Most of it's mine anyhow. (*Pause.*) The boat *is* stopping.
JOSEPH. Get ready to show me that trick. But there's something you—

(*GERHARDT has entered silently. CROSSMAN and JOSEPH notice him simultaneously.*)

GERHARDT. The door was open.
Mr. O'Bannon was in quite a hurry.
CROSSMAN. On his way upstairs to strangle his wife. Better get on up there.
GERHARDT. Poker?
CROSSMAN. Private game.
GERHARDT. Your money too?
CROSSMAN. What do you want, sah?
GERHARDT. You'll be pleased to know Mr. O'Bannon didn't go upstairs. He headed down. To the stalls

probably. Cool off a bit, I imagine, before resuming his game.

Joseph, why don't you go keep an eye on him? Just in case.

(JOSEPH exits.)

GERHARDT. This your deck, Mr. Crossman?
CROSSMAN. It's a house deck, Gerhardt. Ask Joseph.
GERHARDT. I see you are winning this evening.
CROSSMAN. I *was.*

(CROSSMAN reaches for the deck. GERHARDT gets there before him. CROSSMAN is now nervous. GERHARDT examines it.)

GERHARDT. I had a feeling about you, Mr. Crossman.
I was right.
This is not a house deck.
CROSSMAN. You gonna arrest me?
GERHARDT. Regrettably—no. But. You will have to make restitution for the federal statute which you have violated.
CROSSMAN. What statute? What the hell is a statute?
GERHARDT. In this case, an unwritten law. One that says that all cheats must pay duty to a higher authority. *(Begins counting money in Crossman's pile.)* Twenty percent will go to the poor and meek—
CROSSMAN. You sonuvabitch.
GERHARDT. The penny drops, aren't you the quick one—Another twenty to widows and orphans—

CROSSMAN. (*Overlapping*.) You gotta a helluva nerve insinuatin' your oily self in here, putting the screws to me—didn't take you long—

GERHARDT. —And lastly, the law requires a generous donation to create a home, clean, well-lighted, for retired government deputies in their waning years.

CROSSMAN. I got a mind—

GERHARDT. —Oh, cork the indignation, Crossman. The captain will not openly side with his swindlers and you know it. His highly placed friends wouldn't like that. Gotta maintain appearances even if they're no fun.

Make a fuss and you'll put him in the position of having to order me to arrest you.

CROSSMAN. Everybody on the river hates your guts.

GERHARDT. You will find me in the saloon after the game.

CROSSMAN. I could lose.

GERHARDT. In that case, I'll be very disappointed.

(*LIGHTS DOWN.*)

Scene 8

LIGHTS UP on O'BANNON in the stalls. JOSEPH enters quietly. A beat.

O'BANNON. (*Without looking*.) You're following me.

JOSEPH. No sah. (*Pause*.) Yes sah.

O'BANNON. You can go on about your business. I've no intention of making a fool of myself.

JOSEPH. No sah.

(A beat.)

O'BANNON. What do you think of her?
JOSEPH. Who sah?
O'BANNON. The sermon here on four legs. Proportion. Strength. Spirit. Grace.
JOSEPH. She's all that.
O'BANNON. Animals. No way to know what they're thinking. Had a horse once, better-looking than this one. Tried to kill me.
JOSEPH. You going back to the game, Mr. O'Bannon?
O'BANNON. How'd my wife seem to you? Was she angry?
JOSEPH. Angry? I don't know.
O'BANNON. Did she laugh, think her antics funny?
JOSEPH. No sah. Might be she was angry.
O'BANNON. Might be.
First of the month, Mrs. O'Bannon and myself will have been married ten years. That is seven years longer than my first wife, may she rest in peace.
JOSEPH. Good long time to be married.
O'BANNON. I bought this horse for my wife as an anniversary gift. She has not been down to see it one time.
What's that?
JOSEPH. What sah?
O'BANNON. Mare seems to be shyin' off weight on that back leg. Look.
JOSEPH. Where?
O'BANNON. Left back leg.
JOSEPH. Look fine to me.

O'BANNON. Last anniversary I bought my wife a pearl necklace. What does she tell me? She tells me pearls are for funerals.

I could swear—I hope this mare hasn't come up lame.

JOSEPH. I don't see nothing wrong with that leg, sah.

O'BANNON. Ain't even got her home yet.

JOSEPH. Boat's shifting, Mr. O'Bannon, that's all. Nothing wrong with the horse.

O'BANNON. It would be a shame to have to put her down.

JOSEPH. Sah?

O'BANNON. Go back to Mr. Crossman. Tell him I'll be right up.

JOSEPH. Yes sah. (*JOSEPH exits.*)

O'BANNON. (*Spits.*) Pearls are for funerals.

(*LIGHTS down.*)

Scene 9

A clock CHIMES. LIGHTS UP on the O'Bannon stateroom. HAYES and MRS. O'BANNON are once again seated on opposite sides of the table, facing DS. MRS. O'BANNON stares mournfully into her lap. HAYES is decidedly ill-at-ease. Neither looks at the other. A beat.

HAYES. It might be best if I—went. I think. (*A beat.*) Yes, I think—(*HE rises.*)

MRS. O'BANNON. I am so—ashamed.

(SHE covers her face with her hands. HAYES, concerned, but still at a loss, sits.)

HAYES. Mrs. O'Bannon.

Mrs. O'Bannon, there's no harm in your having expressed—what you did. To me. I am—flattered that I—that you feel toward me as you do.

Lord, I wish I had more expertise in such things.

I had no idea. It never even occurred to me that your—that you would—could entertain such a—

(This last does not help matters. MRS. O'BANNON appears to be experiencing considerable anguish.)

HAYES. Is there anything I can get you? A drink of water?

(SHE nods slightly, "no.")

HAYES. You must understand. This is—pure infatuation. Fantasy.

(Another slight nod, "yes.")

HAYES. It can't ever come to anything.

(Another "yes.")

HAYES. Well. Then. Good. Your husband will never know of this, I assure you.

MRS. O'BANNON. Thank you.
HAYES. Soon, you'll—be home. All will be well.

*(Another quiet onslaught of emotion from MRS.
    O'BANNON.)*

HAYES. Oh Lord. I really should go now, Mrs.
O'Bannon.
MRS. O'BANNON. Please. I don't think I can bear to
be alone just now. Oh, I want to die.
HAYES. Oh my.
Well. Mr. O'Bannon might come in. That could be
awkward for you. For both of us, actually.
MRS. O'BANNON. He's not coming.
He wouldn't have come in any event. He doesn't care.
So it doesn't really matter whether I provoke him or no.
HAYES. Uh-huh.
MRS. O'BANNON. He does it at home regularly.
Which I suppose must be the cause of my conceiving
this—infatuation.
You will never forgive me. How could you?
HAYES. Well, of course, I can.
MRS. O'BANNON. I have always prided myself on
being level-headed. Practical. Yet, now look, I've made a
proper idiot of myself. I've embarrassed you. I've been very
selfish. And I am deeply sorry for having made you the
victim of my—ridiculous emotions.
HAYES. Well. That's alright.
MRS. O'BANNON. I am so ashamed.
I don't even know how to explain it.
HAYES. You're lonely. That's all.

MRS. O'BANNON. Yes. I suppose that's it. If that's any kind of excuse.

(A beat.)

HAYES. Well. This is definitely a new experience for me.
George, you see, is usually the one who—

(A pause.)

MRS. O'BANNON. Yes. It seemed to me he likes himself rather a lot, your friend.
HAYES. You think that too?
MRS. O'BANNON. Oh yes.
HAYES. Huh.
MRS. O'BANNON. Forgive me. He is your friend.
HAYES. Oh, but George does fancy himself. It's really irritating.
MRS. O'BANNON. You've been very kind, Mr. Hayes. Understanding and kind.
HAYES. No shame in being lonely.
MRS. O'BANNON. More than sufficient.
HAYES. Well. I do not presume to know how it is with those of the gentler sex, Mrs. O'Bannon.
But, for myself, I'm no stranger to loneliness either.
Or longing.
Such feelings are powerful.
MRS. O'BANNON. Truly.
HAYES. Why, there have been nights, more than I care to number, when I have been laying there—in the

darkness—can't sleep—nobody about—nothing at all to do.

You start thinking, you know, about things. There in the dark. All the getting and doing which only a few hours before seemed so important—necessary—and all of it suddenly loses its meaning. All of it. Days and nights, they just blend together so you can't distinguish one from another. You try to pick 'em out but you can't. So you're left with this—grey ribbon stretching all the way back as long as you can remember. And forward, too, further than you want to imagine. Endless. All the way to the grave.

And there it is. A dull, grey, ordinary thing. Your life.

And so to save yourself, you recall the brighter moments you stored away. Silly mostly.

A small fine hand on the railing. A ringlet that's come loose in the breeze, glinting in the sun. The murmur of a sweet voice through the wall. Scent of lavender water. The rustle silk makes going by. Sometimes it's a face you once tipped your hat to, admired in passing, and thought no more about. Until right then.

Those moments sustain you. And pain you like fire. But they're all you have and somehow, they get you through. Through all the might-have-beens and should-haves-and-didn'ts. All the regrets you now own because it's always been more important to watch the table. And keep your eyes on the god almighty cards in your hand.

(Surprised and chastened, MRS. O'BANNON glances at HAYES. No more pretense now. Gently, SHE reaches out and touches his hand.)

Scene 10

LIGHTS UP on Crossman's stateroom. O'BANNON has lost most of his money and is drunk but holds it well.

O'BANNON. How much is it?

CROSSMAN. You bet two. I matched and raised four hundred.

O'BANNON. Four hundred.

CROSSMAN. Looks like you've come short. I can advance you some.

O'BANNON. No.

CROSSMAN. You out?

O'BANNON. No.

(A beat.)

CROSSMAN. Do we have a plan?

O'BANNON. I'm thinking.

CROSSMAN. You got the time?

(O'BANNON checks his watch and puts it away. A beat.)

CROSSMAN. What time is it?

O'BANNON. Still early.

JOSEPH. Quarter before midnight.

O'BANNON. Is it your impression, Crossman, that Mrs. O'Bannon is—a handsome woman?

CROSSMAN. You're not thinking to bet *her*, I hope.

O'BANNON. I asked a question.

CROSSMAN. Not my place to make that kind of observation, Mr. O'Bannon.

O'BANNON. I just want to know what you think. Man to man. Word around the saloon is you know women, so I ask your opinion.

CROSSMAN. Some might say she is most handsome, sir.

O'BANNON. Another drink.

(JOSEPH pours. As he does, O'BANNON reaches into his boot and pulls out a buck knife.)

O'BANNON. My wife, you see, thinks I'm too predictable. Too much the creature of habit. Always complaining about it.

(O'BANNON has slit the lining of his jacket and now pulls forth a large wad of cash. HE sticks the knife into the table, counts out the appropriate number of bills which HE tosses into the pot.)

CROSSMAN. I'd say you were downright full of surprises.

O'BANNON. Call. Raise four hundred. Anyhow, I find my wife's behavior of late peculiar.

CROSSMAN. Oh, women get their moods. I wouldn't pay it no nevermind.

O'BANNON. So you don't think all this criticism and—disrespect, this moodiness mean anything in particular.

CROSSMAN. Like what—exactly?

O'BANNON. I don't know. I'm asking you.

CROSSMAN. I'm not that much of an expert.

O'BANNON. I'm wondering now if I maybe acted too hastily.

You trust the Reverend?

CROSSMAN. (*A beat. CROSSMAN relieved, laughs.*) Sorry. But that's rich.

O'BANNON. Not his style then.

CROSSMAN. (*Pause.*) Well. You never know.

O'BANNON. You won.

CROSSMAN. What? Oh. So I did.

O'BANNON. There's something amiss. I can feel it. Been married a while, you sense these things.

CROSSMAN. Afraid this'll be the last hand. I'm all in.

O'BANNON. Still early. He's your friend. I didn't mean to offend.

CROSSMAN. I probably shouldn't tell you this—but you did right in keeping him out the game.

He's not really a friend. After me to work with him.

O'BANNON. What's that mean—work with him?

CROSSMAN. He *used* to be a reverend. Now, well, he just uses that. I told him I got a job, thanks.

O'BANNON. He's not a reverend?

CROSSMAN. He earns his living playing cards.

(*A beat.*)

O'BANNON. Thank you for being frank, Crossman. I'm obliged.

CROSSMAN. Thought you oughta know.

Parting drink?

(O'BANNON nods. JOSEPH pours the drinks. CROSSMAN and O'BANNON rise.)

CROSSMAN. Hope the game was to your liking. Even if you didn't go home with my fare in your pocket.

O'BANNON. We got another couple weeks on this boat. Plenty of time.

CROSSMAN. Vote For Ferguson Before Ferguson Dies. Right. Well. *(Toasting.)* To you enjoying the fortune you've already got. To me, enjoying the fotune I've just recently acquired.

O'BANNON. Temporarily acquired.

(THEY drink.)

O'BANNON. At least, you didn't get my horse. And you won't neither.

CROSSMAN. *(Laughs.)* The horse you can keep. You're gonna need it.

Just don't starve this one to death and you'll be jake.

(A beat as CROSSMAN realizes his slip. O'BANNON and HE go for the knife. LIGHTS TO BLACK. A long scream that is the boat's WHISTLE.)

Scene 11

A week later. Crossman's stateroom. JOSEPH straightens and sweeps the room under the following. GERHARDT enters, startling JOSEPH.

GERHARDT. 'Fraid of ghosts?

JOSEPH. Captain told me to clean up. They finished in here.

GERHARDT. Well.

Congratulations are in order.

JOSEPH. Sah?

GERHARDT. One passenger crushed under the wheel. One gone missing with the other's money a mile from shore in twenty feet of water with strong current. On my watch.

Should look fine on the record. And all I could say was, didn't see the fight, sir. Down in the saloon the whole time, sir, having a drink, sir. Enjoying the ride. Sir.

The captain was most sympathetic. (*Beat.*) I wished to heaven I'd never set foot on this Christ-cursed tub.

JOSEPH. Yes sah. (*Pause.*) I mean I'm sorry, Mr. Gerhardt.

GERHARDT. No need. Tomorrow, I take the first steamer north. I've been called back. You'll have someone new.

JOSEPH. Maybe the next post'll be better. More to your liking.

GERHARDT. Maybe. (*Beat.*) Joseph?

JOSEPH. Yes sah.

GERHARDT. I appreciate you not mentioning that I— that I was in here that night. That would have— complicated things.

JOSEPH. Surely.

(*GERHARDT takes a coin from his pocket and offers it to
    JOSEPH who looks at it coolly.*)

GERHARDT. A bon voyage gift.
JOSEPH. Thank you, sah. (*JOSEPH takes the coin.*)
GERHARDT. Well then. I best go and pack.
Better tell the captain to get those busted guards fixed today unless he wants another tragedy.
JOSEPH. Yes sah. He knows.
GERHARDT. Well then. Good-bye Joseph. And good luck.
JOSEPH. Same to you, sah.

(*GERHARDT exits. A beat. JOSEPH looks at the coin in his hand with disgust. HE throws the coin after GERHARDT. A clock CHIMES. JOSEPH takes O'Bannon's watch from his pocket and checks the time. HE replaces the watch, then smooths his coat with his hands, feeling the money sewn into its lining. As LIGHTS SLOWLY DOWN, HE smiles bitterly.*)

Scene 12

The stalls. MRS. O'BANNON in mourning, wearing her pearls, is seated, her face an impassive mask. Enter HAYES. Hat in hand, HE approaches hesitantly. SHE does not acknowledge him. HE clears his throat. Still no response.

HAYES. The captain prevailed upon me to come down and see if you—required anything.

I wasn't sure this was a good idea. Being as how I was the one introduced George to—
Well. He insisted.
So.
How is it with you, m'am?

(*A beat.*)

They say you are refusing to take meals.
You have to eat, Mrs. O'Bannon. You'll make yourself ill. (*A beat.*) The captain wants to call in a doctor. He's concerned.
So am I.
MRS. O'BANNON. You needn't be, Mr. Hayes. (*A beat.*) Tell the captain I am all right.
I have not lost my mind.
HAYES. Then—I may tell him you will eat something?
MRS. O'BANNON. Have they found Mr. Crossman?
HAYES. No, m'am. They have not.
MRS. O'BANNON. Do you believe he's dead?
HAYES. Yes. Yes, I do.
MRS. O'BANNON. You sound very certain of that.
HAYES. George admitted to me once he hated the river. Hated travelling on it. Hated everything about it.
He was afraid of it because he couldn't swim a lick. That's the truth. (*A beat.*) Mrs. O'Bannon, I suppose the real reason I'm here was to tell you—was to confess my responsibility for what occurred—
MRS. O'BANNON. —No—
HAYES. —And I *am* responsible—

MRS. O'BANNON. (*Overlapping.*)—I don't want to hear this—

HAYES. I think you should—

MRS. O'BANNON. No. No. No! (*A pause.*) There is no forgiveness. (*Softly.*) There can be no forgiveness.

(*HAYES moves to go.*)

MRS. O'BANNON. Mr. Hayes.

(*HAYES pauses.*)

MRS. O'BANNON. I understand the desire, the need to share emotions—guilt. But is it wise? Trust is such a fragile thing, better a solitary torment than to risk its destruction. Our suffering is our own regardless. We cannot change what's past.

(*HAYES nods and moves to leave.*)

MRS. O'BANNON. That is not to say—we should be slaves.

We may yet redeem ourselves in pursuing our dreams. The future. That's what's important. Not who we were, or are. But the person we would become.

(*HAYES turns and looks at MRS. O'BANNON quizzically. SHE smiles faintly at him. HE returns the smile.*)

MRS. O'BANNON. Do you know anything about thoroughbred horses, Mr. Hayes?

HAYES. Kind of a lot. Actually.
MRS. O'BANNON. Somehow I thought you might.

BLACKOUT

END OF PLAY

PRODUCTION NOTES

The play is designed to work on a single-unit set with the various locations of the boat designated by lighting (and/or levels) and suggested by an absolute minimum of set pieces. There should be no set walls and a minimum of scene changes in order to facilitate quick and fluid transitions between scenes, allow the audience to see simultaneous action in different locales, and to contribute to the confined atmosphere in which the action of the play occurs.

The American Stage production provided a good example of how the many locations of the play might work. The set was designed to accommodate a proscenium stage with a slight thrust and utilized three basic levels. A stage right level served as the O'Bannon stateroom and remained constant throughout the play. A middle level, stage center, functioned as the saloon dining room, and, in Act II, transformed to Crossman's cabin. A small third level, extreme stage left, served as the saloon bar for the scenes between Hayes and Mr. O'Bannon, and Joseph and Crossman in Act I. The thrust area in front, with various lighting effects, functioned as the deck, and the stalls. Translucent draping served to separate the different locations from one another. Like a scrim, they were front-lit to create the effect of intimacy in the cabins and back-lit when the airiness of the deck or saloon was called for.

COSTUME PLOT

EUGENIE O'BANNON
White cotton chemise
White cotton pantalettes
Large underskirt or crinoline
Corset
Full-skirted gown, dark in color
Full-skirted town dress, somber in color (optional)
Lace fan
Wedding ring
Pearl necklace
Assorted period jewelry (optional)

GEORGE CROSSMAN
Long underwear
Shirt with high detachable collar (1850's period)
Pair of dark-colored trousers with button front
Pair of suspenders
Waistcoat
Cravat
Frock coat of dark color
Pair of boots
Top hat or derby
Handkerchief
Silver card case
Deck of cards

TITUS O'BANNON
Shirt with high detachable collar (1850's period)
Pair of dark-colored trousers with button front
Pair of suspenders

Waistcoat
Cravat
Frock coat of dark color (with basted slit in dark lining for
money)
Pair of boots (one with attached sheath for knife)
Top hat or derby
Handkerchief
Gold watch with fob
Buck knife
Several stacks of large denomination bills (in coat lining)

JACKSON JOHN HAYES
Shirt with high collar (1850's period)
Pair of black trousers with button front
Black waistcoat
Black frock coat
Black pair of boots
Black top hat or derby
A Bible (black)

JOSEPH
Pair of trousers with button front, dark colored and neatly
pressed
Pair of boots, black and highly polished
Starched white shirt with high collar (1850's period)
White cravat
White servant's coat (long and slightly flared, like a frock
coat)
Silver serving tray
A waiter's serving cloth

GERHARDT
Shirt with high detachable collar (1850's period)
Pair of grey-colored trousers with button front
Pair of suspenders
Grey waistcoat
Black or grey Cravat
Grey frock coat
Pair of boots
Grey top hat or derby
Pair of period spectacles

PROPERTY PLOT

ONSTAGE:
The O'Bannon stateroom (SR)
Bed
  Pillows(s)
  Sheets
  Coverlet
2 chairs (DL)
1 small table (DL)
A dressing table with one drawer (DR)
  Jewelry box
  A woman's hair brush

In the drawer or preset on dresser top of Act II:
  A pen
  Paper
  A bottle of ink

A chair for the dressing table
A large traveling trunk with drawers (optional)
A side table
  Pitcher with water
  A bowl
  A sponge or washcloth

The Saloon (Act I, SL)
A small table
  A newspaper
  A glass of whiskey
Two chairs either side of small table
A chair (partially visible UR of other two)

A spittoon

The Dining Saloon (CS)
A dining table
  White linen tablecloth
  Four place settings (knife, forks, wine glasses, serviettes)
  Four matching dining table chairs
A serving table (UR)
  Bottle of wine
  Bottle of champagne
  Bottle of brandy
  3 brandy glasses
  4 plates (preset food)
  A corkscrew
  Water pitcher with water

Mr. Crossman's stateroom (SL area, Act II)
A table
  A deck of cards
  A bottle of Old Monongehela whiskey
  Two glasses
  Two stacks of money
2 chairs
A daybed with coverlet (DL)

PRESET:
A large platter
  A large slice of cheese
  A knife
A novel (Mrs. O'Bannon's)
Playing card in Mrs. O'Bannon's bodice

NEW COMEDIES FROM
SAMUEL FRENCH, INC.

MAIDS OF HONOR. (Little Theatre.) Comedy. Joan Casademont. 3m., 4f. Comb Int./Ext. Elizabeth McGovern, Laila Robins and Kyra Sedgwick starred in this warm, wacky comedy at Off-Broadway's famed WPA Theatre. Monica Bowlin, a local TV talk-show host, is getting married. Her two sisters, Isabelle and Annie, are intent on talking her out of it. It seems that Mr. Wonderful, the groom-to-be, is about to be indicted for insider trading, a little secret he has failed to share with his fiancee, Monica. She has a secret she has kept herself, too—she's pregnant, possibly not by her groom-to-be! All this is uncovered by delightfully kookie Isabelle, who aspires to be an investigative reporter. She'd also like to get Monica to realize that she is marrying the wrong man, for the wrong reason. She should be marrying ex-boyfriend Roger Dowling, who has come back to return a diary Monica left behind. And sister Annie should be marrying the caterer for the wedding, old flame Harry Hobson—but for some reason she can't relax enough to see how perfect he is for her. The reason for all three Bowlin women's difficulties with men, the reason why they have always made the wrong choice and failed to see the right one, is that they are the adult children of an alcoholic father and an abused mother, both now passed away, and they cannot allow themselves to love because they themselves feel unlovable. Sound gloomy and depressing? No, indeed. This delightful, wise and warm-hearted new play is loaded with laughs. We would also like to point out to all you actors that the play is also loaded with excellent monologues, at least one of which was recently included in an anthology of monologues from the best new plays.)　　　　(#14961)

GROTESQUE LOVESONGS. (Little Theatre.) Comedy. Don Nigro. (Author of *The Curate Shakespeare As You Like It, Seascape with Sharks and Dancer* and other plays). This quirky new comedy about a family in Terre Haute, Indiana, enchanted audiences at NYC's famed WPA Theatre. Two brothers, Pete and John, live with their parents in a big old house with an attached greenhouse. The father, Dan, has a horticulture business. A pretty young woman named Romy is more or less engaged to marry younger brother Johnny as the play begins, and their prospects look quite rosy, for Johnny has just inherited a ton of money from recently-deceased family friend, Mr. Agajanian. Why, wonders Pete, has Agajanian left his entire estate to Johnny? He starts to persistently ask this question to his mother, Louise. Eventually, Louise does admit that, in fact, Mr. Agajanian was Johnny's father. This news stuns Johnny; but he's not *really* staggered until he goes down to the greenhouse and finds Pete and Romy making love. Pete, it seems, has always desperately wanted Romy; but when she chose Johnny instead he married a woman in the circus who turned out to be a con artist, taking him for everything he had and then disappearing. It seems everyone but Johnny is haunted by a traumatic past experience: Louise by her affair with Agajanian; Dan by the memory of his first true love, a Terre Haute whore; Pete by his failed marriage, and Romy by her *two* failed marriages. (One husband she left; the other was run over by a truckload of chickens [He loved cartoons so much, says Romy, that it was only fitting he should die like Wile E. Coyote.]). And, each character but Johnny knows what he wants. Louise and Dan want the contentment of their marriage; Romy wants to bake bread in a big old house—and she wants Pete, who finally admits that he wants her, too. And, finally, Johnny realizes what he wants. He does not want the money, or Agajanian's house. He wants to go to Nashville to make his own way as a singer of sad—yes, grotesque—love songs in the night. NOTE: this play is a treasure-trove of scene and monologue material.)　　　　(#9925)

THE BABY DANCE
Little Theatre-Drama
by Jane Anderson

3m., 2f. 2 Ints. Stephanie Zimbalist starred in the original production of this brilliant, moving new drama, both at the Pasadena Playhouse and at the Long Wharf Theatre. She played a woman from Los Angeles named Rachel who has everything she wants in life—except a child. Rachel has located a poor couple who have more children than they can afford to keep, and have agreed to let their latest, when it is born, be adopted by Rachel and her husband. Desperate for a healthy baby, Rachel is paying for all of the poor woman's pre-natal care and hospital expenses. When she arrives for a visit at the trailer park where Al and Wanda live, she is appalled to find that Wanda is not eating correctly. She is also appalled by Al, who actually comes on to her when he is not seething with resentment. The whole arrangement nearly falls through, but by the second act, both couples are back on track. Until, that is, it is learned that the newborn baby may—just may—have suffered some brain damage in the difficult birth, causing Wanda's husband to back away from the deal, much to Rachel's chagrin. Rachel wants the baby anyway, wants to take the chance. In the end, the childless couple do renege on the deal, leaving Wanda and Al with yet another mouth to feed. "The best play produced this season at the Long Wharf Theatre and the first in several seasons to touch the heart so profoundly."—New Haven Advocate. "*The Baby Dance* is not just a 'woman's play.' It is a gripping drama that leaves the audience with more empathy for these people than they would have thought possible."—Bridgeport Post. "A powerful, deeply wrenching drama."—Berkshire Eagle. "It would take a heart of stone to be unmoved by Jane Anderson's *The Baby Dance*.".   (#4305)

THE BATTLE OF SHALLOWFORD
Little Theatre-Comedy
by Ed Simpson

8m., 1f. Int. On a quiet Sunday night, the local regulars have gathered at Burton Mock's general store, in the small town of Shallowford, NC. It is October, 1938. The rest of the world is poised on the brink of war, but the locals aren't much worried about events in the world at large. They're more interested in the local gossip—and Burton's general store is the best place to hear it. The regulars include the gossipy, whining Clunette; fey church choirmaster Fred; lowlife, wild-eyed Newsome Jarvis, on hand with his "slow" son, Doodad; Mr. Roy, a one-armed World War I veteran who holds court at the store; egotistic local football hero Dewey Sowers; Burton's restless young daughter, Ruthie; and her schoolmate Lonny Hutchins, a sci-fi aficionado. All is calm; until, that is, they turn on the radio and learn that the Martians have invaded! Of course, it is the famous Orson Welles broadcast they are listening to—but they fall for it hook, line and shotgun, and run out to do battle against the fearsome threat from the invading Martians. Only Lonny suspects that something is fishy, but he's got his hands full if he thinks he's gonna deter the local yokels from their moment of glory. This delightful new comedy has had several successful productions nation-wide, and is finally available to y'all. Read it if you want a good laugh; produce it if that's how you like your audience to respond. "A theatrical gem."—Asheville Citizen-Times. "Tickle their funny bones, warm their hearts, don't insult their intelligence ... Ed Simpson's *The Battle of Shallowford* hits that magic trio."—Knoxville News-Sentinel. "A sentimental comedy that's hilariously on target. It could easily become a community theatre staple in much the way the works of Larry Shue have."—Knoxville Journal. A cassette tape of excerpts from the Mercury Theatre's radio broadcast of "The War of the Worlds" called for in the text of the play is available for $10, plus postage.   (#4315)

CEMENTVILLE
by Jane Martin
Comedy
Little Theatre

(5m., 9f.) Int. The comic sensation of the 1991 Humana Festival at the famed Actors Theatre of Louisville, this wildly funny new play by the mysterious author of *Talking With* and *Vital Signs* is a brilliant portrayal of America's fascination with fantasy entertainment, "the growth industry of the 90's." We are in a run-down locker room in a seedy sports arena in the Armpit of the Universe, "Cementville, Tennessee," with the scurviest bunch of professional wrasslers you ever saw. This is decidedly a small-time operation—not the big time you see on TV. The promoter, Bigman, also appears in the show. He and his brother Eddie are the only men, though; for the main attraction(s) are the "ladies." There's Tiger, who comes with a big drinking problem and a small dog; Dani, who comes with a large chip on her shoulder against Bigman, who owes all the girls several weeks' pay; Lessa, an ex-Olympic shotputter with delusions that she is actually employed presently in athletics; and Netty, an overweight older woman who appears in the ring dressed in baggy pajamas, with her hair in curlers, as the character "Pajama Mama." There is the eager-beaver go-fer Nola, a teenager who dreams of someday entering the glamorous world of pro wrestling herself. And then, there are the Knockout Sisters, refugees from the Big Time but banned from it for heavy-duty abuse of pharmaceuticals as well as having gotten arrested *in flagrante delicto* with the Mayor of Los Angeles. They have just gotten out of the slammer; but their indefatigable manager, Mother Crocker ("Of the Auto-Repair Crockers") hopes to get them reinstated, if she can keep them off the white powder. Bigman has hired the Knockout Sisters as tonight's main attraction, and the fur really flies along with the sparks when the other women find out about the Knockout Sisters. Bigman has really got his hands full tonight. He's gotta get the girls to tear each other up in the ring, not the locker room; he's gotta deal with tough-as-nails Mother Crocker; he's gotta keep an arena full of tanked-up rubes from tearing up the joint—and he's gotta solve the mystery of who bit off his brother Eddie's dick last night. (#5580)

RAVENSCROFT. (Little Theatre.) Mystery. Don Nigro. 1m., 5f. Simple unit set. This unusual play is several cuts above the genre it explores, a Gothic thriller for groups that don't usually do such things, a thinking person's mystery, a dark comedy that is at times immensely funny and at others quite frightening. On a snowy night, Inspector Ruffing is called to a remote English country house to investigate the headlong plunge of a young manservant, Patrick Roarke, down the main staircase, and finds himself getting increasingly involved in the lives of five alluring and dangerous women— Marcy, the beautiful Viennese governess with a past, Mrs. Ravenscroft, the flirtatious and chattery lady of the manor, Gillian, her charming but possibly demented daughter, Mrs. French, the formidable and passionate cook, and Dolly, a frantic and terrified little maid—who lead him through an increasingly bewildering labyrinth of contradictory versions of what happened to Patrick and to the dead Mr. Ravenscroft before him. There are ghosts at the top of the staircase, skeletons in the closet, and much more than the Inspector had bargained for as his quest to solve one mystery leads him deeper and deeper into others and to an investigation of his own tortured soul and the nature of truth itself. You will not guess the ending, but you will be teased, seduced, bewildered, amused, frightened and led along with the Inspector to a dark encounter with truth, or something even stranger. A funny, first rate psychological mystery, and more.

(#19987)

DARK SONNETS OF THE LADY, THE. (Advanced Groups.) Drama. Don Nigro. 4m., 4f. Unit set. First produced professionally at the McCarter Theatre in Princeton and a finalist for the National Play Award, this stunningly theatrical and very funny drama takes place in Vienna in the fall of the year 1900, when Dora, a beautiful and brilliant young girl, walks into the office of Sigmund Freud, then an obscure doctor in his forties, to begin the most famous and controversial encounter in the history of psychoanalysis. Dora is funny, suspicious, sarcastic and elusive, and Freud become fascinated and obsessed by her and by the intricate labyrinth of her illness. He moves like a detective through the mystery of her life, and we meet in the course of his journey through her mind: her lecherous father, her obsessively house-cleaning mother, her irritating brother, her sinister admirer Herr Klippstein and his sensual and seductive wife, and their pretty and lost little governess. Nightmares, fantasies, hallucinations and memories all come alive onstage in a wild kaleidoscopic tapestry as Freud moves closer and closer to the truth about Dora's murky past, and the play becomes a kind of war between the two of them about what the truth is, about the uneasy truce between men and women, and ultimately a tragic love story. Laced throughout with eerie and haunting Strauss waltzes, this is a rich, complex, challenging and delightfully intriguing universe, a series of riddles one inside the other that lead the audience step by step to the center of Dora's troubled soul and her innermost secrets. Is Dora sick, or is the corrupt patriarchal society in which she and Freud are both trapped the real source of a complex group neurosis that binds all the characters together in a dark web of desperate erotic relationships, a kind of beautiful, insane and terrible dance of life, desire and death?

(#5952)

TWO NEW COMEDIES FROM
SAMUEL FRENCH, Inc.

FAST GIRLS. (Little Theatre). Comedy. Diana Amsterdam. 2m., 3f. Int. Lucy Lewis is a contemporary, single woman in her thirties with what used to be called a "healthy sex life," much to the chagrin of her mother, who feels Lucy is too fast, too easy—and too single. Her best friend, on the other hand, neighbor Abigail McBride, is deeply envious of Lucy's ease with men. When Lucy wants to date a man she just calls him up, whereas Abigail sits home alone waiting for Ernest, who may not even know she exists, to call. The only time Abigail isn't by the phone is after Lucy has had a hot date, when she comes over to Lucy's apartment to hear the juicy details and get green with envy. Sometimes, though, Lucy doesn't want to talk about it, which drives Abigail *nuts* ("If you don't tell me about men I have no love life!"). Lucy's mother arrives to take the bull by the horns, so to speak, arriving with a challenge. Mom claims no man will marry Lucy (even were she to *want to* get married), because she's too easy. Lucy takes up the challenge, announcing that she is going to get stalwart ex-boyfriend Sidney ("we're just friends") Epstein to propose to her. Easier said than done. Sidney doesn't *want* a fast girl. Maybe dear old Mom is right, thinks Lucy. Maybe fast girls *can't* have it all. "Amsterdam makes us laugh, listen and think."—Daily Record. "Brilliantly comic moments."—The Monitor. "rapidly paced comedy with a load of laughs . . . a funny entertainment with some pause for reflection on today's [sexual] confusion."—Suburban News. "Takes a penetrating look at [contemporary sexual chaos]. Passion, celibacy, marriage, fidelity are just some of the subjects that Diana Amsterdam hilariously examines."—Tribune News. **(#8149)**

ADVICE FROM A CATERPILLAR. (Little Theatre.) Comedy. Douglas Carter Beane. 2m. 2f. 1 Unit set & 1 Int. Ally Sheedy and Dennis Christopher starred in the delightful off-Broadway production of this hip new comedy. Ms. Sheedy played Missy, an avant garde video artist who specializes in re-runs of her family's home videos, adding her own disparaging remarks. Needless to say, she is very alienated from the middle-class, family values she grew up with, which makes her very *au courant*, but strangely unhappy. She has a successful career and a satisfactory love-life with a businessman named Suit. Suit's married, but that doesn't stop him and Missy from carrying on. Something's missing, though—and Missy isn't sure what it is, until she meets Brat. He is a handsome young aspiring actor. Unfortunately, Brat is also the boyfriend of Missy's best friend. Sound familiar? It isn't—because Missy's best friend is a gay man named Spaz! Spaz has been urging Missy to find an unmarried boyfriend, but this is too much—too much for Spaz, too much for Suit and, possibly, too much for Missy. Does she *want* a serious relationship (ugh—how bourgeois!)? Can a bisexual unemployed actor actually be her Mr. Wonderful? "Very funny ... a delightful evening."—Town & Village. **(#3876)**

OTHER PUBLICATIONS FOR YOUR INTEREST

COASTAL DISTURBANCES
(Little Theatre- Comedy)

by TINA HOWE

3 male, 4 female

This new Broadway hit from the author of *PAINTING CHURCHES, MUSEUM,* and *THE ART OF DINING* is quite daring and experimental, in that it is *not* cynical or alienated about love and romance. This is an ensemble play about four generations of vacationers on a Massachusetts beach which focuses on a budding romance between a hunk of a lifeguard and a kooky young photographer. Structured as a series of vignettes taking place over the course of the summer, the play looks at love from all sides now. "A modern play about love that is, for once, actually about love--as opposed to sexual, social or marital politics . . . it generously illuminates the intimate landscape between men and women." --NY Times. "Enchanting."--New Yorker. #5755

APPROACHING ZANZIBAR
(Advanced Groups—Comedy)

by TINA HOWE

2 male, 4 female, 3 children --Various Ints. and Exts.

This new play by the author of *Painting Churches, Coastal Disturbances, Museum,* and *The Art of Dining* is about the cross-country journey of the Blossom family--Wallace and Charlotte and their two kids Turner and Pony--out west to visit Charlotte's aunt Olivia Childs in Taos, New Mexico. Aunt Olivia, a renowned environmental artist who creates enormous "sculptures" of hundreds of kites, is dying of cancer, and Charlotte wants to see her one last time. The family camps out along the way, having various adventures and meeting other relatives and strangers, until, eventually, they arrive in Taos, where Olivia is fading in and out of reality--or is she? Little Pony Blossom persuades the old lady to stand up and jump up and down on the bed, and we are left with final entrancing image of Aunt Olivia and Pony bouncing on the bed like a trampoline. Has a miracle occurred? "What pervades the shadow is Miss Howe's originality and purity of her dramatic imagination."--The New Yorker. #3140

Other Publications for Your Interest

THE VOICE OF THE PRAIRIE
(LITTLE THEATRE—COMIC/DRAMA)
By JOHN OLIVE

2 men, 1 women—to play a variety of roles
May be done with up to 10 actors—Unit Setting

When this play begins, we are listening to an old hobo (named "Poppy" by his avid companion young Davey Quinn) tell a tall tale. It is the early 1890's, and itinerant story tellers such as Poppy really were the voices of the prairie. Many years later, when Davey is grown up, he is "discovered" by radio entrepreneur Leon Schwab, telling his tales of Poppy and of Frankie the Blind Girl, whom he rescued from a cruel father and with whom he went on a cross-country adventure. Schwab thinks Quinn's stories would attract an audience for radio, the "wave of the future". Sure enough, David Quinn becomes famous as the Voice of the Prairie, as the cleverly-constructed play cross-cuts between scenes of Leon and David and scenes of young Davey and Frankie the Blind Girl, on the lam, in search of adventure. These scenes culminate in the unfortunate separation of Davey and Frankie, as Frankie is recognized, captured and sent back home. David Quinn, the grown-up Voice of the Prairie, has not seen or heard from her since; until, that is, Leon locates her in hopes of using his discovery of the actual, famous Frankie the Blind Girl for its sentimental value, to keep the new F.C.C. off his back. Will David forgive Frankie for leaving him so many years ago? Will Frankie agree to help Leon avoid jail for broadcasting without a license? "Endearing."—N.Y. Times. "That rare thing: a small, skillful play with a deft heart."—Los Angeles Times. "Beguiling entertainment and as American as corn."—Hartford Advocate. "First-rate entertainment. I can't remember when I last so enjoyed a play."—Torrington Register Citizen. Slightly Restricted.

(#24047)

CARELESS LOVE
(LITTLE THEATRE—DRAMA)
By JOHN OLIVE

1 male, 1 woman—Unit set

What a terrific little play for an actress and actor to sink their teeth into! And, it's about something that matters: committment, and responsibility, in love. When we first meet Jack, he is an aspiring actor, serious about his career but not very serious about his girlfriend, Martha, a waitress who is an aspiring dancer, who is a lot more serious about Jack. The couple drifts along on a cloud of good times — until Martha gets pregnant, at which time a *Choice* must be made. As the debate over their options progresses, Jack's acting career starts to take off; and, he starts to think more seriously about his life and his responsibilities. Unfortunately, at the same time Martha has been driven into self-absorption by Jack's carelessness, and has made a decision which is right for her, she thinks: she has decided to give the child up for adoption. So — at just about the time Jack is ready to make an emotional committment to Martha and to their child, it is too late: Martha has had the baby and put it up for adoption. This was, after all, *her* decision to make. Right? In the end, Martha is a self-sufficient contemporary woman, who makes her own choices. It is Jack who will hurt forever, from the pain of eternal separation from his child. "Bittersweet." — Variety. "In the delicacy of its writing, in the truth of its details...it is a most lovely, most satisfying evening in the theatre."—Chicago Tribune. "A lovely little play...works a winsome magic."—Philadelphia Daily News.

(#5237)